How the bee got inside my bib overalls

and other

FARM STORIES

from the Forties & Fifties

By Harry Macomber

George Macomber

"Building the Harness exhibit"

See the Macomber Harness Exhibit
**in the carriage barn of the
Sutherland-Wilson Farmstead Museum,
797 Textile Road, Ann Arbor, Michigan**

•

Pittsfield Township Historical Society
P.O. Box 6013, Ann Arbor, Michigan 48106

Or on the Web @www.pittsfieldhistory.org

Published for the
Pittsfield Township Historical Society
by Pierian Press

Proud dad

Daughter Melanie, Dad Harry, Son Adam

Dedicated with heartfelt thanks

To Julie
This book and these stories would not exist
had our paths not crossed. I am forever grateful they did.

To Mom & Dad
You were the inspiration and guidance. Thank you.

To Jerry Holthouse
for the cover design
and the technical expertise from the crew at Buford Lewis

And special thanks to Tom Dodd
and to the Pittsfield Township Historical Society

-Harry Macomber

Pittsfield Township
Historical Society
2005-2006 Board

Visit us on the Web @
www.pittsfieldhistory.org

Pittsfield Township Historical Society
P.O. Box 6013
Ann Arbor, Michigan 48106

Foreword

Harry Macomber came back to Michigan to sit down around a farmhouse table with members of the Pittsfield Township Historical Society. He was looking for a place to put his father's tack—two sets of harness that his father had used his entire adult life. Reflecting his father's pride in caring for those harnesses all those years, Harry was looking for a permanent home. The old barns at Pittsfield Township's Sutherland/Wilson Farmstead Museum seemed the perfect place to preserve and display them.

Pittsfield's team of Doug, Doug, and Don (Woolley, Kettlewell, and LeClair) don't spend much time sitting around the table at this old farm. They are usually armpit deep in restoration projects on the property. But this day was different.

Four guys sitting around a table in a farmhouse eventually gave way to story-telling and Harry Macomber had lots of stories to tell. He told of growing up on a farm at 6844 Park Road, just west of Ann Arbor, Michigan. And he told of a later farm the family operated on Sharon Hollow Road near Manchester. And he told of his current horse farm near Watertown, Tennessee.

Harry is a farm boy with vivid memories of a slower paced, very caring stewardship of the land when family farms were truly that. Harry had already written several stories when the meeting with the Pittsfield guys took place. They encouraged him to write enough for a book. Here they are.

The Pittsfield Township Historical Society thanks you for your support of the Sutherland-Wilson Farmstead museum. Come on over and see Harry's magnificent tack display in the carriage barn.

And be prepared to listen to—or tell—farm stories.

The author with a prize Duroc - 1955

FARM STORIES

Three generations of the Macomber family: George, Harry, Adam; Manchester Fair Parade, 1996

Silence is golden

We are surrounded today by power tools—electric or battery operated. They perform a multitude of tasks making it easier and faster to complete any project our minds can imagine. When people observe me using old-fashioned hand tools, they're quick to remind me how much faster and easier it would be if I used power tools. I simply answer that I like the quiet and feel of doing things by hand. They are usually at a loss for a response to that and only smile and nod their heads.

Our noisy world today blocks out so many natural sounds that I grew up with—mostly the sounds of birds, insects and frogs of all kinds. As I drove to work today I was remembering many of the tasks we did on the farm, all by hand. They involved many hours of hard, repetitive labor, but the reward was the atmosphere we did them in. It may have been hard on the muscles, but it was great for the spirit.

One such example was opening the cornfield for harvest. Farmers did whatever necessary back then to avoid wasting crops. We would cut the outside row of corn by hand all the way around the field. On the headlands, near the gate where we entered, we'd cut back several rows for turning. All this was done to keep the horses and heavy corn binder from knocking down and wasting any stalks as they started the harvest.

The only tools needed for this job were a sharp corn knife and some binder twine. The stalks of corn would be taller than I was and an inch or more in diameter at the base. As I swung the corn knife with my right arm, I'd catch the falling stalks in my left arm until I had more weight than I could drag. I'd lay the stalks down and start again. After cutting several bundles, I'd go back and tie each one once around the middle. I'd then stand them up against the fence, out of the path of the horses and corn binder. We'd add them into the corn shocks later.

I grew to love that kind of quiet labor and still do today: the wet dew still on the leaves of the stalks, the sun slowly rising and the temperature with it; the sounds of the birds and all manner of insects creating a symphony free and uninhibited; a slight breeze and white, puffy clouds drifting slowly overhead against the blue sky. I miss those days that never hurried. Cutting thistles, pulling mustard, and building fence were other jobs that were done quietly by hand. In the 1940s, especially, when horses were still the main power source, so many days were filled with only the sounds of nature. No motors intruded.

Dad didn't believe in getting modern too fast, as my siblings will all concur. He was the last one to give up his team of horses and use tractors. During oat harvesting time, even after we got the modern Case combine, we still unloaded the oats into the granary with shovels and buckets. That was an after-breakfast and chores job. Dad would fill the wood rack of the one and a half ton stake truck each afternoon. Usually 250 to 300 bushels were waiting to be unloaded into the granary the next morning. My two older sisters and two younger brothers and I would stare at that mountain of oats with dread. Dad would be mowing hay, cultivating corn or greasing the combine for the afternoon's combining, so unloading fell to us kids.

Our granary stood on legs and the floor was the same height as the truck bed. We'd start by reaching over the end gate and dipping out buckets of oats. Once we'd dipped out all we could, one of us would crawl in and fill the buckets and hand them out. We'd have to unload about fifty buckets before we had a spot cleared enough to remove the center section of the tailgate. Then we could walk in and fill our buckets and shovels and walk into the granary and throw it into the bin Dad had designated. This job consumed most of the morning as our enthusiasm about finishing quickly slowly diminished. Even our sibling conversation or complaints slowly gave way to silence broken only by the scraping sounds of our buckets and shovels.

Hoeing in the garden, pitching hay in the mow, even many of our daily chores were done without the aid of any motorized helper.

Silence is not only golden, it's also a big part of developing character and giving lift to the human spirit. We can do things faster and easier now, that's true, but the ugly by-product of that is stress, something that wasn't present those long ago summer days in the 1940s.

•

I offer these short stories as a window to the world I was privileged to be born into. Yes, nostalgia creeps in and colors our memories of our past. But most of what I've written here is an honest portrayal of those events. It was hard physically because of the extensive hand labor, but I'd live it all again, the bad and the good.

We should each remind ourselves what a privilege it was for most of us to be born in this country. We are inundated with images of people around the world and all manner of suffering. We are indeed among the lucky few.

Grandad standing on top of the thresher

The bee inside
my bib overalls

My encounter with the bee, still a vivid memory today, taught me no great lessons in life unless, of course, it was to have a healthy respect for—and perhaps still some fear of—flying, stinging insects, especially their single mindedness once they zero in on a target. If I learned anything that day, it was the realization that bumblebees have absolutely no sense of humor! I remind my own son of that each time we encounter one in the fields or woods.

I remember it was in late summer, probably August. It was wheat-threshing time. Weeks before, the tall golden grain had been cut and bundled in the field by teams of horses pulling grain binders. The bundles had quickly been shocked in neat rows across the field to cure. Likewise, the oats which usually matured just behind the wheat. Not many farmers owned one of the big grain threshers for separating the wheat from the straw. The one who did hauled it from farm to farm. It would rumble slowly down the road, the steel wheels of the thresher and tractor pulling it leaving behind a strange pattern as the steel cleats dug into the hard gravel. It was a favorite time for me. I was five or six that year; old enough to appreciate all that was going on around me, but too young to actively take a part in the hard physical labor involved. By the time I was big enough, modern combines pulled through the fields had replaced the threshers.

My grandfather owned the thresher that sat on the barn hill of our farm that long-ago day. A long wide belt ran down to the tractor, which powered it. The back of the thresher sat inside the barn, its front wheels up on planks to level it from end to end, an important factor in effectively separating the grain from the chaff as it shook and shimmied from several sheaves to the screens below. A built-in fan blew the light husks from the kernels of grain. Dust and debris constantly floated in, around, above and below the pulsating, vibrating monster. A long round blower pipe, big enough for me to crawl though if I'd had the nerve, extended out the back door of the loft. The bent and broken stems of the once tall wheat exited at the end of the pipe. Two men below, with three-tined pitchforks, moved and stacked the straw as it cascaded down in gold volumes. The golden stack of straw, carefully squared at each corner, rose foot by foot. A wooden ladder was soon carried out and leaned against the stack so the men could descend and get a much-needed drink while a new wagonload of bundles was pulled forward.

On the side near the rear of the thresher were some smaller pipes. These carried the clean kernels of wheat into a bagger attached to the side. Tall, gray cotton bags, each holding three bushels of grain, were waiting nearby. Two men manned this station also. The bags were as tall as I was. It took strong men to lift them off the baggier, pull a string from their back pocket and, in one fluid motion, tie a miller's knot around the neaty gathered top. Some were carried untied and dumped into a bin in the granary located on one end of the loft. I'd crawl into the bin, sinking several inches into the soft sea of kernels. I'd take a small handful of the wheat, check for live bugs, and then pop it into my mouth. I liked the taste of the sweet, crunchy kernels of wheat. I'd only eat a couple of mouths full though, as Dad had warned me each year that any more was likely to give me a first class bellyache. I had no intention of spoiling one of my favorite days of the year, to say nothing of the tasty meal my Mom, sisters, and aunts were preparing as we men quietly worked together.

My grandpa, whom I'm named after—and the only witness later that day as I danced with a live bee sharing the space inside my bib overalls—always fed the bundles into the thresher himself. He was a wisp of a man in stature, but a giant in the eyes of the men who struggled to match the pace he set for the entire crew. My dad was bigger and stronger than my grandpa, but he remained in awe of his dad, reminding me years later of the reputation I had to match if I was to do justice to my namesake. But that day, the reputation I would build as a worker was far from my mind. Threshing only happened once a year and my only wish was to be in a half dozen places at the same time so I wouldn't miss any of it. There was so much to see and do.

I'd hitch a ride on the wagon with Dad as he trotted the horses back to the field for another load. I'd hold the reins of the horses as I stood on the front standard of the wagon. I wasn't really driving, since the horses were following Dad's verbal commands as he neatly stacked the bundles down both sides of

the wagon, but it was fun to pretend I was. Two men walked beside the wagon as we stopped briefly at each shock of wheat. The three-tined forks flashed in the sun as the shock, bundle by bundle, quickly transformed from ground to wagon. Dad would yell, "Giddup."

I'd add my command and give the lines a flick across their backs as I'd seen Dad do, and we'd move on to the next shock. Two bundles would already be in the air toward Dad by the time he hollered "whoa." When we finally had a load, I'd be standing on the second board from the top, bundles of wheat surrounding me on three sides. I could barely move, but at least I wasn't in danger of falling off. Dad would sit on top of the load, his feet dangling over the front beside me. He'd take the lines, a quick flick of the reins and we were headed to the barn.

One of the few regrets I have about those times is that modern tractors came along ten years too soon. I never got to establish that unspoken understanding with horses that the men of my dad's generation and before had. A team in the hands of a good horseman was merely an extension of his own arms. It was enjoyable to watch—all that power responding to those two thin, black lines and a few verbal commands.

When it came to driving horses, my dad had few equals. I've seen his team back a four-wheel spreader through a barn door with only two inches total space beyond the wheels. He'd get off the seat and walk beside the horses; their only clue was his voice commands. The horses, themselves, could only see forward as the blinder beside each eye, built into the bridle, kept them from being distracted by activity around them. This was done as much for their safety as for the driver's. It also developed a deep trust in the team as they relied solely on the driver for directions.

By the time I turned ten, Dad had purchased a small Farmall tractor. Sitting on the seat—a steering wheel instead of reins—was where I spent the next two years farming. By twelve I was driving the bigger tractors—rubber-tired monsters that had lost their original steel wheels to the welder's torch.

By the time Dad and I arrived at the barn, it was dinnertime. Men back then would not be late for meals. When the food was pulled hot from the oven or scraped from the skillet, the men were at the table ready to eat it. To do less would dishonor the time and special effort the women put into preparing it. What a meal it was! The women at each farm knew the men would all go home and tell their families about the meal they'd had at dinner that day. No effort was spared to satisfy the hunger the hard morning's work had produced.

I also enjoyed watching the men wash up and comb their hair before coming into the house for dinner. As I've indicated, threshing was a dirty job. The men's faces and arms would be dark with sweat, dust, and dirt. Those men working beside the great metal thresher were covered in dirt and chaff. The two men working on the straw stack were likewise a much darker shade.

On the lawn near the house under the spreading limbs of a giant elm tree, Dad had placed Mom's wash bench and two large square wash tubs. They were filled with water. There were towels and hand washbowls on another bench. Each man, in turn, would pick up a washbowl, dip it half full of water from the tub, and sit it on a bench. Bars of Lava soap were soon dipping into the quickly darkening water; hands, arms, then face and neck all got equal treatment. The dirty water would be thrown under a nearby bush and clean rinse water would be dipped out. After a thorough rinse, the washbowl passed to the next in line. Dad made me wait until the men were all finished. I'd watch as they dried their arms and face on the big burlap towels. A few combs were nearby and a small mirror that usually hung in our washroom was now hanging from a limb on the elm. Woven amongst all the activities was a constant banter discussing the success of the morning, the yield per acre, the weather, and the price of wheat at the mill. I was at the 'seen and not be heard" age, but I was so caught up in listening that voicing my opinion had never occurred to me. I still believe to this day that kids who are taught to listen, watch, and think for themselves are much more prepared for life than those getting instant answers to every question. When it was finally Dad's and my turn, we had to hurry, as no one would enter the house until Dad did.

If possible, Mom would try to squeeze me in beside Dad at the big dining room table; every extra leaf had been inserted in the center of the table to accommodate the threshing crew. To my eyes it looked as big as the wagons we hauled the bundles on. My Mom and her "crew" started the big bowls of food at one end nearest the kitchen. What a feast it was. If a bowl emptied before it got all the way around, another was substituted without a pause. And there were pies—one of the few times during the year that I had to make a choice as to what kind I wanted: cherry, apple, rhubarb, custard, lemon. No skinny six-year-old boy, already full of mashed potatoes, roast beef, and lima beans should have to make that choice, to narrow it down to one. It just wasn't fair! Almost as if a whistle had blown, the men would all get up and head outside again, each nodding and complimenting the ladies on a fine meal as they passed.

The sun had passed its high spot, allowing our tall silo to start casting its shadow across the tractor and the singing belt powering the thresher. All the barns where I grew up were two stories. On the ground floor there were the stanchions that held the cows while they were milked. A ramp of dirt was built so that the wagons could be pulled or backed up into the barn floor above. It was a long dirt ramp, so as not to be too steep for the horses to pull the loaded wagons up its grade. Grandpa's big steel-wheeled tractor sat part way up the ramp. There was room for the teams and wagons to pass it as they pulled up beside the thresher. Once they were unloaded, the skilled teams would back the empty wagon back down the ramp to where they could turn around and head back to the field. There was a fieldstone wall built on each side of the ramp to hold the dirt in place.

A team and wagon had just left and the next one had not appeared around the corner leading to the lane. Grandpa climbed down from the thresher and slowed the big tractor to an idle. He stood there impatiently waiting. I was on the ramp, walking up the wide top of the stones that held it. There was some grass and a few weeds growing right next to the wall. This was the stage upon which I was about to do my impromptu, unrehearsed dance. One weed in particular caught my attention; it was a big tough one—what Dad referred to as "pig weed". At this point in the summer they had toughened and dried to the point of being almost indestructible.

Before I relate how what happened next was possible, I better clarify how I was dressed. I had on a pair of bib overalls, just like Dad's. I had a cotton shirt on, and shoes and socks. Underwear had not entered the dress code and wouldn't until I started attending the big city school in junior high. Since my skinny frame didn't come close to filling out those bib overalls, there was plenty of air circulation between them and me. I can best describe myself as looking like a small scarecrow on a stick after all the straw stuffing had fallen out. I was built just like Grandpa.

I grabbed on to the pig weed with both hands. I'm not sure why, really; maybe just because it was there or because it stood out above all the rest. I bent it, twisted it, and gave it a couple of tugs to no avail. I reached lower down on the main stem with both hands and braced my legs. That weed was coming out! I gave a mighty jerk! I almost lost my balance and fell backward as the dry dirt released the weed. Dust and dirt flew up into my face as the tough roots gave way.

Before I could revel in my triumph, I heard the dreaded buzz of an unhappy bumblebee. I dropped the weed and looked down. My first mistake was not using that time to turn and run. I saw a moving flicker of yellow down among the grass and weeds. Still, I didn't move. I am by nature slow to panic. This was about to become one of those rare exceptions. Then it was quiet and the buzzing stopped. Before I could dwell on the meaning, I felt the faint breeze of beating wings on my bare leg below the knee. I'm not sure which happened first, the jumping or the hollering. Maybe it was one of those rare times in my life where my coordination was perfect.

All I know for sure is that I was suddenly airborne and hollering at the top of my lungs. I jumped and hollered, twisted and turned. That bumblebee, flying blind in the dark interior of my bib overalls, was having his own troubles bumping and buzzing his way higher and higher. Then I made my second mistake. I started tying to hit him through my bib overalls each time I felt his legs touch my skin.

Looking back, I realize that there was no good way to remove that bumblebee from inside my clothes without getting stung at least once. If sheer force of movement could have shaken him out. I had given it my best shot. Suddenly my chest felt the fiery sensation I had struggled mightily to avoid. I grabbed my bibs and shirt and pulled them out from my chest. That bumblebee saw daylight at last and he was gone.

Tears of fear and pain were pouring down my cheeks. I looked around. Grandpa was roaring with laughter. I guess the look on my face must have finally touched him as he came running over to where I stood. He helped me get my suspenders off my shoulders and open my shirt. There, almost perfectly positioned between the nipples on my chest, was a growing, burning, red bump. My whole chest was throbbing and on fire.

Grandpa, I would realize over time, was the last one you'd call on if you were looking for sympathy, especially for something as trivial to him as a bee sting. After getting me calmed some, he sent me to his house to see Grandma. There, I got a hug and some baking soda to help soothe the sting.

I've gotten stung several times since that day, especially during haying season when we'd disturb the nests hidden in the grass. I never cried after that but, to this day, I give bumblebees the right-of-way any time our paths happen to cross.

George raking hay

Hayin' time

Molly and Dolly, Dad's favorite team of sorrel workhorses, waited patiently as he adjusted the tugs and neck yoke. The fly nets on their backs swayed as they tossed their heads or raised a leg occasionally to drive off the pesky, ever present flies. They were already sweaty, having been in the fields early raking hay with the John Deere side-delivery rake.

Dad was now hooking them to the hay wagon. We had time to get a load before dinner (that being the noon meal, supper was in the evening).

My sister Shirley, the oldest of us kids and the only one experienced at driving a team, came running from the house. She loved the outdoors and especially horses. She wouldn't miss out on any chance to drive. I was too young yet, but I got to go along to learn. Having finished hooking up the team, Dad stuck the lines through the boards of the front standard for Shirley. He then jumped on the wagon, took the reins, and "chirped" to Molly and Dolly. A flick of the lines and we were on our way.

The front standard was around seven-foot high; two oak two-by-fours for upright and one-by-six boards spaced about eight inches apart. Two slings hung over the top of the two-by-fours which extended a few inches above the top board. The back standard was only about three feet high, just a couple of boards. One sling was already stretched out over the bed of the empty wagon. There was a metal ring on each end where the long ropes came together.

Two-by-two wooden slats about four feet apart held the ropes in place. At the very center of the sling the ropes came together. There was a metal trip mechanism that locked them together. A long slender rope to trip the sling and drop the hay ran over to the side of the wagon and hung over the edge. It must swing free as the hay was pulled up into the mow so Dad could hook his three-tine pitchfork into the metal ring and trip it.

We headed down the lane. I realize looking back, why the days seemed so long then. Farmers worked hard, for long hours, as they do now, but there were the little "time breaks" like this of silent contemplation. The horses walked quietly down the sandy, partly grassy tracks in the center of the lane. Dad didn't trot them. They'd already put in three or four hours of work.

The dull thud of the horses' hooves in unison, the jangle of the tugs, and creaking of the wagon, all were background to a suspension of time. Dad in his bib overalls and summer straw hat, his long sleeved shirt rolled up to the elbows, the reins held loosely in one hand. Shirley and I stood on either side hanging onto the front standard looking at the horses, or maybe orange and black meadowlarks or Lassie trotting along side. There was just no way to hurry this moment, no way for technology to cut that precious time on that particular day.

When we arrived in the hay field, Dad guided the team and wagon back to the hay loader. Those awkwardly shaped machines were marvels of ingenuity. It towered above even the front standard of the wagon. It had two large steel wheels that carried all the weight and two small ones that swiveled and kept the loader in balance. It had a very short tongue, so it rode almost against the back of the wagon. A big round group of bars low to the ground with tines extended, picked up the winrow of hay. As it came up and around, it was squeezed between moving ropes and taken to the very top. Then it cascaded down a short chute onto the wagon; the chute was adjustable so at the start the hay would fall down onto the empty wagon. As the load got higher, Dad would raise it until, at the top of the load, it was pushing it almost straight up. I was fascinated most by the fact that the winrow of hay stayed in exactly the shape that it lay on the ground, as it was picked up and carried to the top of the loader. Not until Dad's three-tine pitchfork moved it around the wagon did the winrow finally lose its shape.

Shirley and I had to soon start climbing the front standard to avoid being covered up with hay. Dad would move large forkfuls expertly around the wagon as we rolled slowly across the field. When we had a third of a wagon full, Dad would yell, "Whoa." We'd stop while Dad grabbed another sling, swung it around the edge of the front standard and spread it out across the loose hay. It was done carefully since the success of getting the big slings of hay up to the barn roof and safely through the big door, depended on Dad's skill at spreading the hay and centering the sling on the wagon. Shirley had been driving a team loading hay since she was four. Now, at around twelve, she could guide the team around the corners of the field so that the loader back behind the wagon still followed the center of the winrow as it made the turn. This meant guiding the team outside the winrow as they started into the turn. She'd already had lots of practice in knowing how far out to go to keep the loader centered.

By the time dad was putting the final touches of hay on top, Shirley and I were mostly hidden from his view. We were against the front standard still, but dad had surrounded us with hay until it loomed over our heads behind us. We both had necks full of chaff by then which worked itself down inside our shirts. From somewhere up on top we'd hear dad's "whoa". He'd slide down the back of the load, hanging onto the loader and unhook it. Then he'd come around to the front, climb the standard and seat himself on top of the load, his feet resting on the very top board. Shirley and I would stay where we were. It was safe there, even if the jiggling of the wagon over the ground brought fresh cascades of chaff down our necks.

Then it was another long, slow walk back to the barns. Every life should contain times like those. There was never much conversation. Dad would usually have a stem of hay he was chewing on. I'd try to imitate him by carefully picking myself out a stem of Timothy. With a rein in each hand he'd guide us slowly through the gates, the load so wide it brushed the posts on each side.

There was closeness in farm families, a sense of purpose, of shared appreciation that needed no conversation to confirm.

Dad parked that big wagon of hay right below the door of our horse barn. Certain fields of hay went into the barns that contained the animals the hay was more suited for. After dinner it was time to unload the hay. It seemed such a long way up to that ten-foot by twelve-foot door at the very peak of the barn's end. A metal track that ran the length of the barn extended out about six feet. A "car" with four metal wheels sat at the very end. A rope extended down with a pulley and two large hooks.

Molly and Dolly waited patiently

The rope ran all the way back to the other end, down the outside of the barn to another pulley, then back the length of the barn to our Dodge stake truck. It was hooked by clevis to the front bumper. This heavy, thick rope is what pulled the slings up to the door above and into the mow. Dad would give the rope slack so it came down and rested on the hay. The two hooks and pulley gave it weight. One hook went to each end of the sling and into the iron rings. Dad would put the big truck in reverse and start back. By hooking to the front bumper, dad could watch all that was happening as he pulled the sling up into the barn.

Shirley and I, per our instructions, stayed well back in case the rope broke. Dad was never a hugs-and-kisses person, but our safety and well-being never left the very top of his priorities. Farms are dangerous places for kids.

As Dad started back, the two ends of the sling would draw together, gradually making a big ball of hay. Once they met, the sling would start going up. The rope would creak as the heavy hay stretched it tight. Once the pulley and hooks attached to the sling bumped the "car" at the top, it would release the brake and the sling, swaying back and forth, and would disappear into the barn. On rare occasion the sling would be accidentally tripped as it lay on the wagon. The two ends would slide out from under the hay and start up empty. Dad would have to pitch off some hay by hand and hope the next sling could take a little extra weight as it was pulled up.

I'd follow Dad up the ladder to watch him trip the sling. I don't know how many pounds of hay were in a sling, but I know it was enough to crush and cover Dad and me in an instant——especially if we were just starting to fill the mow. That huge mass of hay hung enormously above us, still swaying slightly.

Loading hay

There was no way to lower it once the car had tripped and started rolling into the barn.

There were two small ropes tied to each end of the car; this allowed Dad to position the hay wherever he wanted—way back to the far end or just inside the big door. Dad would take his three-tined fork and stick one tine through the ring at the end of the trip rope. A twist of the fork and he was ready. If the mow were already partly full, he'd simply jerk and the hay would come crashing down and spread back out as it had been on the wagon. The two halves of the sling, still attached at the car, would swing wildly for a moment. If we were just starting, as we were that day, Dad would try to position the hay toward one side or the other of the wide barn. He'd pull gently on the trip rope and start the big sling swaying—wider and wider; at its furthest point he'd jerk the rope.

When I got old enough to work in the mow, Dad would let me trip the sling; I'd jerk and run. The hay falling behind me would create a small gale of wind and chaff that would sweep over us each time. That short time of fun was followed by a good fifteen minutes of hand-pitching the packed hay to the outside of the mow. It was hot up there! Our shirts would be wet when we climbed down to pull up the next one.

On this particular day, while Dad was in the mow, Shirl and I had to pull the slings back out to the end of the track. We'd both have to pull on the rope together to get enough speed up so it would catch in place at the very end. Then we would carefully lower the empty slings onto the wagon. Our other job was to pull the long heavy rope back to the front of the truck, ready for the next pull. We did this first so we'd have slack enough to lower the slings.

It sounds slow and complicated, trying to describe it all these years later, but it went remarkably smooth.

Dad took good care of all his tools and equipment. There were annual times of the year for greasing and oiling the hay car, the windmill, etc. There was always a grease gun in the tractor toolbox and an oil can hooked on various tools for daily greasing.

By my mid-teens we had switched to baling all our hay and straw. An elevator moved the bales up into the mows. The hay cars sat unused, on the track, cobwebs slowly covering them. The hay loader was hauled to the woods and parked. Somehow its shape to this very day always reminds me of a giant grasshopper, sitting ready at any instant to hop into the air.

A load of loose hay

Mom & Dad

Dad with grandpa's horses

George Macomber,
   October 7, 1909-2000
Mabel Graden Macomber
   August 4, 1914-2003
Shirley (Sparks),
   May 12, 1936
Barbara (Harvey),
   August 29, 1938
Harry,
   July 12, 1940
Carl,
   July 23, 1944
George Jr.,
   April 3, 1946
Linda (Brannick),
   July 1, 1952

6844 Park Road, Ann Arbor

Mom

Mom and Dad, 1934

Before & after: 65th wedding anniversary

Whipporwill Farm, 8720 Sharon Hollow Road, Manchester

The McCormick Deering 10-20

Plowing with the 10-20

My foot struggled to push in the stiff clutch on the McCormick Deering 10-20. I was trying to slip the clutch a little as the front wheel entered the furrow. Holding the metal steering wheel with both hands for leverage against the resistance of the clutch, I eased the big tractor forward until the ribbed rear tire entered the furrow too. I let go of the clutch and reached back with one hand and quickly jerked the rope that tripped the two-bottom plow and sent it burrowing into the ground.

I was plowing, on my own, all alone on the tractor! I pulled the throttle back to the notch Dad had shown me. I glanced back. Dad was standing, watching. I quickly turned my attention back to the front tire that was riding the inside edge of the last furrow Dad had plowed moments before. I dared not let that tractor's tires veer right or left and mar the straight furrows Dad had already turned.

It was the fall of 1952; I was 12 years old and still well shy of a 100 pounds, even soaking wet. I had driven the 10-20 before, pulling a four-section drag or a disc, and even earlier, when I shared the seat with my older sister hauling hay. It had taken both our right feet, hands braced on the steering wheel, to depress the clutch while Dad spread open another sling on the hay wagon.

Here I was, at last, doing the most important part of the fieldwork all by myself. I was plowing.

Turning the rich earth on our Lower Michigan farm had been a favorite part of farming even before I took the wheel myself. I had ridden occasionally, sitting on the big inside fender as Dad expertly guided the tractor around and around, the band of rich, dark earth getting wider and wider with each pass.

I should point out that my Dad and Granddad were perfectionists when it came to plowing though the furrows would soon disappear under the rollers of the culti-packer or the teeth of the drag, both men wanted their furrows straight and clean.

Dad was one of the few farmers who used a combination of a rolling coulter and jointer. The thin, sharp coulter sliced a straight, clean line through the sod, cornstalks or whatever was on the surface. The jointer, a miniature of the plow point, rode against the coulter and turned about five inches of the soil before the plow point and moleboard finished turning the earth into the furrow beside it. The result was a sea of brown, clean furrows with not a weed, stalk or stubble showing.

Dad took great pains in adjusting each part of the plow until it laid the clean, even furrows he wanted. He would point out with great disdain the fields of any neighbor whose plowed field showed the tips of weeds, stalks or stubble sticking out above the top of each furrow. He also set the plow depths to pull up just a little subsoil each time and work it into the rich topsoil. The object was to increase the good soil a little each year. He always checked to make sure I was doing just that.

The old 10-20 moved steadily down the furrow. It sported rubber tires now. A torch had cut off the wide metal bands with thin bolted-on cleats and a metal rim was welded in their place. The rear tires were filled with chloride to increase traction. The front wheels were used car tires. That made turning the big tractor hard for a twelve-year-old boy. Many times I'd turn on the plowed ground and then be unable to straighten out the wheels, I'd have to stop and back up, then start again. They also slid easily at the end of a row as I turned while tripping the plow to bring it out of the ground. To this day, there are steel posts, long ago rusted off at the ground, that have a curve the size of those front tires where I didn't make the turn and didn't get that stiff clutch depressed fast enough.

The barking of that four-cylinder engine was deafening. There was no muffler. The exhaust came right from the manifold on the side of the engine. The metal seat was made for a 200-pound man. I couldn't make it flex even when I jumped on it. An old dirty cushion helped some.

There were no individual foot brakes. A hand lever brake stood beside the shift lever. Even Dad couldn't pull it hard enough to hold the tractor on a hill.

There were three speeds forward, one reverse. I was plowing in second gear. Both right tires rode down in the furrow so the driver was constantly on a slant until they came to the end and turned.

A twist clevis held the plow to the flat wide draw bar on the tractor. A trip rope attached to the rear of the tractor seat by a metal clip.

The plow, also a McCormick-Deering rode on three steel wheels. The one I was now pulling slowly across the field had two fourteen-inch bottoms. It was all the 10-20 could pull in the occasional clay ground of our slightly rolling farmland.

When I reached the far end of the field, I slowed the 10-20 to an idle. Since I couldn't turn the wheel with one hand and trip the plow with the other, correlating the exact spot where the plow left or entered the ground was a little tricky. I was determined to keep those ends even, just like Dad did with such ease. I turned the steering wheel with both hands, then held it with one and reached back and tripped the plow. The tractor continued straight forward, front wheels sliding, despite my turning, until the plow points were almost clear of the ground.

Free of the plow pressure, the tractor would turn normally. Slipping the clutch again as I started back down the other side of plowed ground, I tripped the plow and pulled back the gas throttle I glanced back with great satisfaction as my plow entry matched Dad's perfectly.

I looked to where Dad had been standing. He was gone. I was on my own in a field almost a half mile down our lane from the home and barns. I was not afraid; what I lacked in size and strength, I made up for in determination. The word "can't" was not in Dad and Mom's vocabulary. It would not be part of mine.

There was one advantage to the hard steering and old car tires on the front of the 10-20; it would follow the furrow by itself all the way across the field. By turning the steering wheel slightly so that the front tire was trying to come out of that deep furrow, you could let go of the wheel completely. The friction on the inside of the tire against the still firm, unplowed side of the furrow was enough to hold it steady. I'd seen Dad get off the seat and sit on the fender, giving the tractor more traction on the high side. He'd ride there from one end to the other.

Since our ground varied from clay hills to black marsh soil, it was necessary to adjust the plow lever occasionally while on the move. Dad would simply reach back with one hand, squeeze the handle and move a notch up or down. I couldn't of course. I'd let the 10-20 continue down the furrow while I stood up and turned around, so I could put both hands on the plow lever and move it. By the time I finished that first head-land, I was confident enough to ride the fender like I'd seen Dad do.

It seems to be an unusual truth that turning the soil, whether by hand, by horse or modern tractor, gets into the soul of a man. I believe that's true. It can be addictive.

I can still hear that old 10-20, smell the fresh turned soil and recall all the sights that go with it. As I sat on that fender watching the furrows turn, a small world was in motion around me. The soil was rich with life. Earthworms by the thousands, quickly burrowing back into the soft earth. The white grubs, propelled by a few feet right behind their orange head, were much slower to respond to being suddenly unearthed. They made fat, easy targets for the swarm of birds following me around the field, the songbirds, meadowlarks and blackbirds keeping pace on the fresh earth until their bellies were full.

Swallows swooped and dived on all sides of the moving tractor as grasshoppers and other winged insects took flight from our path. Field mice and an occasional rabbit or pheasant disappeared into the fencerow or marsh.

Farming in the 40's and 50's was land friendly. No chemicals bleached or soured the earth. Crop rotation was standard procedure. It kept the soil rich and fertile and pests such as corn borers low in numbers. Fresh manure was spread in the fields all winter and plowed under in the spring. Corn stalks, likewise, were chopped up by the disc, then plowed under. Generations of farmers had perfected management of the soil to a fine art.

Weeds, thistles, wild carrot, wild mustard, all were either cut with a corn knife or pulled up by the roots each spring and summer. The organic matter plowed under in spring and fall kept the soil not only fertile, but loose so that moisture could get down into the roots of the growing crops. Erosion, never a big problem on our farm, was kept in check by simply tripping the plow out of the ground in the places in danger of forming a gully.

The land was a farmer's very lifeblood; it was treated that way. I know I shared the heartbreak of thousands of other farm boys in the '30s and '40s who see the once fertile fields grown over with weeds, fences gone and sprawling subdivisions obliterating any remnants of the fields so carefully tended during the years we grew into men.

I left my dad and brothers on the farm to pursue a printing and newspaper career. In the mid-1990s, after a series of setbacks, the two farms of my Dad's and brothers' were lost. Before all the legal proceedings were completed, Dad wanted to plant a field of oats. I volunteered to plow and fit the ground in preparations for planting. The tractor I climbed into had little resemblance to the old 10-20. It had a cab, radio, air conditioning and power steering. A long six-bottom plow trailed out behind. It hadn't been used in years. Still I looked forward to once again dropping those two right wheels into the furrow and watching the earth turn behind me.

My brothers had years before switched over to the modern methods used today. No-till and sprays had replaced the plows and cultivators of my youth. The only survivors of the years of spraying seemed to be the thistles and burdocks. They stood out starkly in a landscape turned brown by sprays.

Dad, in his late 80s then, helped me hook the big plow and grease it. I headed the big tractor out to the field. The little levers beside the seat controlled the huge plow behind me. Undaunted, I set the plow into the ground as black smoke rose from the exhaust of the big diesel. I steered straight across the field, knowing Dad would check how straight my furrow was.

I sat in the wide cab on that soft seat and watched out the window as the earth turned behind me. When I turned at the far end and headed back, I wondered where the birds were. None had appeared to feed on the bounty awaiting in the fresh earth. I leaned next to the window over the huge rear tire and looked down at the furrows I had just turned. From that height it would be hard to see the earthworms, but I should be able to spot the fat, white grubs. I could see nothing.

I stopped the big tractor, climbed down the steps to take a closer look. Then it was clear why there were no birds. There were no earthworms, no grubs. In fact, as I walked over the soft, fresh soil, I could detect no life at all. I climbed back into the cab and continued plowing. I felt lonely and, worse, felt deserted. I could be plowing on the moon for the absence of life around me.

I plowed in one day what would have taken me three or four days with the old 10-20. None of the joy I had expected to feel came. We planted the oats and they grew. So did the thistles, with a vengeance

I do not believe in the prophecies of the Bible in Revelations. I cannot accept such a God-induced plague of humans suffering and agony. Instead, as I view the direction we are heading with the production of the food that sustains us all, I can't help wonder if we are creating our own Armageddon— one gallon of spray at a time.

The Case combine with the Dodge stake truck

The new Case combine

I still marvel at the invention of the sickle bar and reel that enabled the grain binders and later combines to harvest the golden grains we grew on our Michigan farm in the mid twentieth century.

I'd sit on the seat of the old McCormick-Deering 10-20 in low gear, almost at an idle, as the heavy Case combine trailed behind, devouring the tall stems of wheat. The sickle knives had their own unique sound and rhythm—so quiet and smooth, and of course deadly, in their task of slicing anything standing in their path. Age and wear would eventually alter their smooth motions to a loud clatter over the years.

As I watched the grain fall to the canvas right behind the sickle laid down by the silent slats of the reel as it turned slowly above, it occurred to me that the sickle did the dirty work. It cut unmercifully the once-growing, living wheat. The reel seemed gentle by comparison. Like a soldier would ease a dying comrade to the ground, the reel would softly, quietly lay the once-tall grain onto the canvas below.

From there, the unsuspecting stalks were a split second from total destruction. The canvas striped with thin slats, seemed oblivious to its part in the deadly work. Continually moving, always upward, it threw its victims into the flailing arms that lay hidden in the darkness just out of sight.

The rest of the job of separating the tiny kernels of wheat from the straw and chaff was done in secret. Belts sang, arms moved, shafts turned, chains rattled on the outside of both sides of the big combine. The only evidence of the *coup de grace* going on inside was a steady flow of clean, reddish brown kernels of wheat dropping into the twenty-five bushel hopper.

Out the back, beaten and shaken until they'd released every kernel of wheat in their heads, the broken, bent stems of straw, fell gently to lie atop the stubble almost at the exact spot they had stood gently swaying in the breeze only seconds before.

My dad had purchased the Case six-foot combine in the early '50s. It was as close to an actual big metal thresher that he could find. Big it was; wider, larger and a lot taller than the neighbors' Massey Harris or John Deere six-foot combines. In fact, it was so big and heavy that the tongue holding it to the rear of the tractor had to be welded and reinforced several times over the years. The original would twist and bend when on a slight hill or crossing a dead furl not filled enough at planting time with the four-section drag.

Balanced on two large wheels, it would push the old 10 – 20 slightly sideways if we turned while going down an incline. On the plus side, it did a wonderful job of cleaning the wheat. We'd get the least cleanings back from the mill after selling our load as any farmer in the long line waiting to unload. It took over an hour each morning for Dad to grease the dozens of grease zerks that dotted the gears chains and pulleys.

On top sat a big gray Wisconsin Motor. I don't recall the horsepower, but it took a strong arm and agile balance to hand crank it to get it started. One long lever beside the hopper started all the humming, shimmying and shaking of the big machine. The lever simply lowered an idler pulley onto the drive belt and we were ready.

In spite of the constant dust and noise, I loved to operate the big machine. I'd gladly stay in the field and miss supper while Dad and my brother milked and did chores.

I was in my mid teens when Dad finally let me operate the combine alone. Wheat was our "cash" crop: we sold most of it straight from the field. We saved a bin full in the granary for the chickens and next year's seed.

Morning dew was a daily occurrence in Lower Michigan where we farmed. It dictated our schedule. Combining, for instance, couldn't start until 11 or 11:30. We'd usually only make a round or two in the field before stopping for dinner.

As the day wore on, it got dryer and the dust drifting up from the moving combine got thicker. We carried a short broom, stuck in a slot at the top of the hopper. When we stopped to unload the grain, part of our routine was to sweep off the hot motor where chaff collected. There were occasional fires each summer where the collected chaff caught fire and burned some farmer's combine and part of the wheat field too. Dad was definitely a preventive maintenance person with the care he used and instructed us kids in.

The evening dew would start as soon as the sun dipped below the horizon; about 7:30 you could hear the subtle difference in the motion of the combine. It made the motor work harder as the slender stalks got damp—it was time to quit for the day.

I'm glad the big Case had a motor of its own. To this day I am still uncomfortable with p.t.o.-driven machinery. I'm uneasy somehow with keeping the r.p.m. in the tractor at a high enough speed to meet the requirements of the machine behind. I don't feel in control of the safety of the tractor under those conditions.

No matter which of our four tractors we hooked to the Case combine, I could gear it so that it quietly pulled the combine at the right speed. Keeping the tractor motor noise down also let me hear any problems occurring in the combine. Things like a squeaky belt or the combine motor being overloaded were easy to detect.

In the low marshy areas, the wheat would get so tall— the heads so heavy before harvest—that a strong gust of wind would lay it permanently on the ground. We were lucky that our land had few rocks. We could lower the head of the combine to within an inch off the ground and scoop up most of the downed wheat.

It was a different story with the oats. They competed with the ragweed every year. Since they ripened a few weeks later than wheat, the ragweed would get within a few inches of the heads, especially in a wet year. This increased the work of our Case combine. More than once we were forced to combine before the oats were at a safe storage moisture because of the ragweed. We'd unload them on the big barn floor and every day Dad and I would turn them with scoop shovels to aid drying before finally carrying them to the bin in bushel baskets.

Years later Dad finally hired a man with a big self-propelled combine to harvest our wheat. Our herd of prize Holstein's was growing so large that our time was taken up with baling extra hay. We also needed more acres of corn. In addition, the show circuit started in July with the *State B&W show*. We were getting a reputation for having show winners so that also took an increasing amount of our time.

It fell on me to take our Dodge one-ton truck to the field and drive up beside the self-propelled combine so he could unload. A few times I'd see Dad come to the field and study the ground behind the big combine. He was looking for kernels of wheat that had ended up on the ground instead of in the hopper. He'd shake his head in disgust, but never said much about it to the combine operator. It was the price to be paid for not taking the time to do it with our old six-foot Case.

Dad finally traded the big Case combine as part of a deal for a new D-17 Allis-Chalmers tractor. It may have been big and cumbersome, but that Case did the best job of combining I've ever seen.

Dad, Harry, Carl, and George Jr., with the Case Combine

Corn husking in the '40s

I never learned to love corn husking like I did threshing wheat and oats. Maybe because it took place in the cold early winter and the stalks and ears of corn were harder to work with.

The corn binder was a marvel to a small boy like I was in the early '40s. It had one wide, giant drive wheel and a skinny one opposite for balance. Two pointed snouts straddled the row of corn. It was a hard machine to pull across the field and required more frequent stops to rest the horse.

Sharp, stationary blades at the base cut the tall stalks. They traveled up to the binder by means of chains, top and bottom, to hold them in a standing position. A bundle would quickly gather, an arm would dart out and loop it with twine, other arms ejected the tied bundle and it fell heavily to the ground.

If the corn were thick, the bundles would lay just feet apart littering the field.

Neighbors would build tall shocks out of the bundles. Each would grow to five or six feet in diameter before another was started. A strand of binder twine would be tied around near the top to keep the wind from dislodging the outside bundles. Our old corn binder, unused for 50 years, still sits quietly in Dad's tool shed. Once the field of corn was transformed to rows of shocks, they were left to dry.

Harvesting the cut corn might be only weeks later or left until mid winter. Sometimes snow would cover the field before the neighbors returned with wagons and teams.

Grandpa would set the corn husker on the same barn hill as he had the wheat and oat thresher a few months before. Sometimes a separate stack of shredded corn stalks would be blown next to the straw stocks in the barnyard below. Sometimes Dad would place the stalks into one of the half-empty haymows on either side of the barn.

Like the thresher, my grandpa fed the stalks into the machine himself. Before I was born, an uncle had lost his hand to a corn husker. Feeding the bundles of stalks seemed much more dangerous to me than gently tossing the bundles of wheat or oats into a thresher.

Grandpa had on heavy winter clothes and gloves or mittens to keep his hands warm. He also had a homemade blade in one hand for cutting the twine just before the bundle was swallowed whole by the giant machine.

The knife consisted of a single blade from a mowing machine. It was bolted to a short handle. Twine ran through a hole in the handle and looped around Grandpa's wrist to avoid losing the knife into the husker—a dangerous combination at best.

I remember one year's corn-husking session in particular because of what I did that day. It was early winter. The ground was frozen and all the critters that lived out of doors were hibernating or nested in warm nests in trees or underground. Corn stalks became winter quarters for hundreds of field mice. Not only were they warm and protected inside the big stalks, but they had an abundant supply of corn for food close at hand. They'd use the corn silk from the ends of the ears for building nests, sometimes raising a litter of babies in their winter mansions. Little did they suspect that these lavish quarters were only temporary.

As the teams and wagons moved through the rows of stalks, men would pitch the bundles one at a time up on the wagon. One man would stack so the big loads would reach the husker without losing any bundles. The mice would scurry to the very last bundle as the shock disappeared from over their heads.

Once that last bundle left the ground, the mice would race for a nearby shock or disappear under the wagon. I decided to catch a few of the smaller mice for pets. Obviously, I didn't consult Mom and Dad on this project. I took a jar with a lid to the field with me. I'd catch one and put them in the jar. They tried to bite me, of course, but I had on a pair of mittens with a pair of gloves inside. I was perfectly safe and it was even fun to watch their little teeth bite into the mittens. By noon I had a dozen or more.

I found a wire screened box about a foot wide, two feet long and a foot tall, in the shed. It had a small opening on the top with a hinged lid. Perfect I thought! I'm not sure what the pen had originally been designed for—maybe pigeons or Bantam chickens. At any rate, I dropped my moving catch inside.

I put an ear of corn in for food and some corn leaves and silk for hiding in. I wanted them to be comfortable in their new surroundings. I even put in a can cover of water so they could drink.

After dinner I started collecting mice like I was on a mission. If I found a nest of babies, I'd carefully put them in my coat pocket while I continued to catch the adults and drop them into my jar. I remember I provided lots of laughs for the men watching me scurry after the darting mice. For every one I caught, I probably missed a dozen or more. I lost count by mid afternoon but knew I had at least a 100 or more by the time we quit for the day.

I put my collection on the back porch and went to do the evening chores. When we came in for supper later, I stopped to check on my mice. The inside of the cage was a beehive of activity. Mice of all sizes were making nests, eating or just scurrying about checking out each other and their surroundings.

Dad came over to see what I was looking at. He had been shoveling corn all day into the crib and hadn't known about my collecting foray until now. He was not amused or appreciative. Neither were my mother and older sisters. I quickly discovered, the only happy ones were me and my contented community of mice.

To my horror, Dad began discussing ways to dispatch my little village. His ideas involved cats and worse.

We finally compromised. I was to free my captives back to the wild that very night, no ifs, ands or buts.

With great reluctance, I put on my hat and coat and carried the cage out to the garden. I couldn't bring myself to dump them out in the cold with no food and water. I tipped the cage gently on its side and opened the door. I stood back and watched.

One or two bigger mice darted out and disappeared into the grass and weeds. I left it to them. When I checked the next morning after chores, the cage was empty.

I did get one more lecture though, when Mom discovered I had freed them only a few feet behind the house. For days she watched for signs that they had moved into the basement and taken up residence with us. None showed up and I could finally breathe a sigh of relief for I would have been the one she made take the trap outside and dispose of the dead, stiff bodies.

That was about the last year we cut and shocked corn. Corn pickers took their place. Mounted on a tractor or pulled behind, the pickers were much quicker and a lot less labor intensive. I, for one, didn't regret seeing those stalks stay in the field. Anyone who has had to feed cattle cornstalks with a four-tined barley fork knows what I mean.

The buzz saw

*The buzz saw
hooked up to the tractor*

Keeping warm in winter
in the '40s and '50s

Every Saturday was wood cutting day!

The aroma of that fresh baked cinnamon bread wafting clear out to the washroom as I entered made me forget for a moment my frozen fingers and nose. My wet gloves, partly iced around the edges, landed on the flat metal heat register near the hallway. Cutting wood every Saturday on our Michigan farm was an unwelcome chore as winter wore on. The reward was that first bite of hot cinnamon bread with icing dripping off the edge. A little butter hastily spread and you were ready for the second part of the Saturday wood fest: Unloading the big stake truck full of wood into the basement.

Saturday was wood cutting day all winter long. We kids were all home from school to help and our big two-story farm house consumed that big truck load of wood every week in the dead of winter. Between morning milking and chores and evening milking and chores was wood cutting time. We used a home-made buzz saw powered by our McCormick-Deering 10-20. The buzz saw was bigger than any of our neighbors' saws. The blade was at least 30 inches in diameter. It had a big table that glided forward as Dad shoved the wood into the blade. When it had finished the cut, a spring would bring it back to the starting position. A wood shield completely covered the blade for safety when the table was all the way forward. The entire saw sat on two runners. Dad added an axle and two iron wheels later for moving it when there was no snow. The top area was around five feet by six feet. Part of the top was stationary.

We boys would struggle to keep feeding buzz sticks to Dad as he worked the table back and forth. The small limbs he insisted we group in two or three at a time. They were for the wood cook stove Mom still preferred over getting an electric one. (She later compromised when Dad found one that still burned wood on one side but had electric burners on the other.)

Our wood-burning furnace seemed like a monster to me. Huge pipes snaked out in all directions. You could throw 14" diameter chunks of wood through the big door with room to spare. On the plus side, that saved us lots of hours splitting the wood into smaller chunks.

Back at the woods, my brothers and I struggled to get the heavy pieces of wood up on the buzz saw table. Dad helped, but once he started sawing, it was up to us to hold it there. Not only did we have to hold it up and level, but we had to move forward in unison as the blade bit into the wood. If we let our end sag or moved forward too fast or too slow, it pinched the blade. A severe pinch would send the belt running back to the 10-20 off the iron pulley that powered the blade. The six-inch-wide belt would flop off wildly into the snow. That meant a ten-minute delay while we reset the 10-20 and retightened the belt.

Like most farmers of that era, Dad put up next winter's wood a year ahead. He'd create buzz piles wherever trees had fallen from old age or wind or ice. Early spring and late fall when field work was at a minimum was the time to put the wood into buzz piles. Our woods was comprised mostly of oak—red, white and black— with some hickory and maple mixed in. During the '40s, when I had not reached my tenth birthday, Dad cut most of the fallen trees with a crosscut saw and axe. I'd try and help but I was doing little more than hanging onto that wood handle for dear life as Dad worked that saw back and forth. I became an expert brush-piler though. Dad insisted on a neat pile, all limbs going the same direction, a lesson I've recently passed on to my youngest son, Adam, who just turned 16. In the mid-'50s, Dad purchased his first chain saw, a heavy, bulky McCollough. Still, for many years, he used the saw for cutting buzz sticks only. When winter came, we simply moved the buzz saw from one pile to the next.

Each Saturday as we prepared to head for the woods

with the 10-20 and dodge stake truck, I'd try to round up as many pairs of gloves as I could. Sometimes I'd double them up in a futile attempt to keep my hands dry and warm. We'd sweep the snow off the buzz piles and shovel a path to walk but, within moments of holding the buzz sticks for the saw, my gloves would be wet. It didn't seem to bother Dad in the least. I'd soon be curling my fingers up inside my gloves or mittens as I walked to get more wood.

That brings up a fond memory from those days—the side manifold exhaust on that old 10-20. I'd run up beside the roaring tractor and hold both hands a couple inches from that hot exhaust. Ah! Did that feel good to my frozen, wet fingers. The hot fumes bounced off my glove and warmed me all over. Dad would continue sawing short sticks until I'd get the look that told me it was time to get back to work. My time in front of that "outdoor heater" was never long enough.

It took at least a couple of hours to fill our one-and-a-half-ton truck. Dad would usually let me drive the truck back while he drove the 10-20. Our farm lane from the woods to the barn was over 3/4 of a mile long. Dad's face would be red from the wind as he drove the slow-moving tractor back. The heaters in trucks back then weren't anything to brag about either, but at least I was out of the wind. Fully loaded, the stake truck was unstoppable in snow. I'd turn slightly back and forth on the return trip so the tires would cut into the snow banks lining the lane. I felt I was driving an army tank that could go through anything.

After our "Cinnamon bread" break, we had to unload the wood into the basement. We'd "bounce" the chunks down into the window well where they'd roll on into the basement. Sometimes, if we were late getting back, we had to milk first and unload the wood after all the chores were done.

My wake-up call for many years was the sounds coming through my upstairs register at five in the morning. I'd first hear Dad move the big lever on the grate back and forth several times to give air to the fire. Then I'd hear the big chunks of wood tumble into the fire to the clank of the hinged fire stopper just inside the furnace door. The basement stairs were right below the stairs leading to the second story where I lingered in my long underwear beneath the flannel sheets. I'd follow the sound of Dad's footsteps as he climbed the basement stairs, go down the short hall and pause at the door leading upstairs.

"Harry! Time for chores." I'd crawl out and reach for my flannel shirt and bib overalls lying beside the warm register.

Silo filling in the 1950s

Along with threshing and corn husking, filling the tall wood silo every summer required the help of neighbors. Not a big crew like for wheat-threshing, silo-filling was usually only shared with one or two close neighbors. Once new tractor pulled choppers replaced the corn binders and teams pulling wagonloads of bundles to the waiting silo filler, the labor required dropped off dramatically.

Two brothers, Harold and Lauran Diuble did custom silo-filling. One pulled the chopper in the field, filling the wagons, the other ran the blower which propelled the silage falling from the back of the wagon, up a pipe and into the silo. Filling our tall wood silo usually took one-and-a-half to two days, depending on how well things went.

The corn was chopped green. We'd wait until the ears were well formed and the bottom of the tall stalks just starting to turn a little brown, indicating the corn plant had reached maturity. The chopped silage was heavy. It took special heavy-framed wagons with oversized tires to carry the silage to the silo.

When the Diuble Brothers first arrived at the farm, we set up the blower. The pipe came in sections that had to be bolted together until it reached the very top of the silo. At the top, a curved spout was guided through the small window in the roof of the silo.

Dad would crawl up the outside of the empty silo through a chute. Inside the chute were individual doors which were put in one-by-one as we filled and, over the course of fall and winter, taken out one-by-one as the silo was emptied. It was a risky job.

Once Dad had carefully made it to the top, he had to shimmy across a plank from the chute to the window. He would carry a long, heavy rope draped across his shoulder, which he put through a pulley and lowered to the ground. It was used to pull the heavy metal pipe in position.

I know it was scary because, when I got older, Dad sent me up to do this task. As I'd shimmy across the plank, I couldn't help but look down inside the silo. It was a long way down to the cement floor. It would be a fatal fall, of that I am sure.

Once I'd lowered the rope down and guided the spout

through the window and it was tied, I'd shimmy backwards across the plank. The ground never felt so good as when I finally stood on it once again.

Ours was a wood stave silo. The boards ran vertically, about an inch thick and six to seven inches wide, grooved to lock together. It was ten to twelve feet in diameter and thirty-five to forty feet tall. Metal hoops held it in its circular shape. They were close together at the bottom where all the pressure would be from the heavy, wet silage—only six inches apart at the bottom, but three feet apart near the top.

Several guidewires of heavy cable held the silo upright. They could be adjusted, if needed, should the silo start leaning one-way or the other. It did just that a few times while I was growing up and we even feared it would come crashing over a couple of times.

Once we had the blower in place, Harold would head to the cornfield to start chopping. Soon the wagonloads would be arriving in a steady stream.

The silo sat right next to the main dairy barn. The barn hill or ramp leading up to the second floor was right beside the silo on one side. We'd set the blower on the ramp as it took less pipe and power to blow the heavy silage into the silo. The wagons had tall sides and held several tons.

A conveyor attached to the blower could be lowered to the ground right behind the wagon. The rear gate would be raised and long-handled silage forks would be used to bring the silage down into the conveyor, which quickly took it into the large blower fins.

It went up the narrow pipe with considerable force; this was a two-man job. Lauren Diuble was there to start and stop the blower and hook silage. Whoever the tractor driver was that pulled up the load was the other.

Inside the silo were three or four men. Another flexible pipe of short sections was hung on the inside. This was so the cascading silage could be positioned evenly around the interior. One man held and guided the pipe. The others were "trampers" and around we went taking short steps, packing the wet silage as tightly as we could. The better job we did of packing, the less settling would occur over the next several days. If the packers did a good job, there was no need for the Diubles to return in a couple of weeks and "cap off" the silo which could settle three to four doors' worth (approximately 10 –12 feet).

When we were filling our own silo, my job was usually driving the Farmall C and pulling the loads of silage up to the

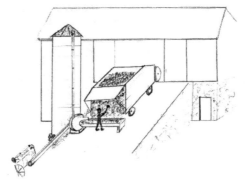

blower. When I helped the neighbors, I usually ended up tramping around and around the silo.

We'd joke and make small talk enclosed in the dark silo. When the silage was coming down the pipe, you couldn't hear conversation; during the brief time the blower was slowed to an idle while a new wagon was pulled up, we would take advantage and swap stories.

The big wagons were equipped with moving chains on the bottom. A small electric motor was attached. As it turned, the silage was slowly transported to the rear of the wagon. There the two men keep hooking it off into the conveyor, pacing it to keep an even flow moving into the spinning blower.

After the silo was filled, the packed wet silage would go through a "curing" process. Foam would seep out between the cracks and ooze down the sides of the silo. The more airtight the silo, the better. If air got into the silage it would mold. This happened around the edges some each year. As we fed the silage over the course of the year, we'd have to throw away small chunks of silage that had spoiled.

During the cold winter months, the silage would freeze around the edge of the silo. We had to chip it off and throw it down the chute each day. It melted once it got down into the warm barn.

Throwing down silage was one daily job I did the most, usually toward the end of the evening milking. We took off four to five inches each time. Dad made sure we took it evenly each time, learning to leave the center a little higher, to keep spoilage to a minimum.

The quiet and isolation inside the silo made it a great place to think as I'd carry forks full of silage over and toss them down the long chute. It was a great place for a teenage boy to deal with all he was learning and thinking as he emerged into manhood.

The Macomber farm at 6844 Park Road

Dairy barn
Sheep
Trucks
Granery
Tool she
Horses
Chickens
Brooder house
Well & milk house
Windmill
Park Road
Hogs
Original house
Garden
Lane
Hog shelter

Building and yard uses at the farm

The barns burned in the early '80s

The house in 1920...

...and in the 1970s

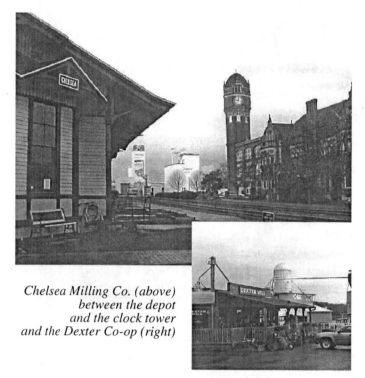

*Chelsea Milling Co. (above)
between the depot
and the clock tower
and the Dexter Co-op (right)*

Taking wheat
to the mill

Like most farm boys of the '40s and '50s, I'd had my hands on some kind of steering wheel since childhood. Driving tractor was a daily part of life, usually starting on Dad's lap when we were kids. We farm boys would be the envy of most kids today. We could have a legal permit to drive on the highways at fourteen. That's how old I was when Dad let me take the Dodge one-and-a-half ton-stake truck, filled with wheat, to the mill to be sold.

The Chelsea Milling Company was about fifteen miles away. That was the usual destination each year for our wheat, which was our "cash" crop. On rare occasions, if the line at Chelsea Milling was too long, Dad would go instead to the Dexter Co-op. They usually paid a few cents less per bushel, but the line to unload was always shorter. Dad had to weigh the slight difference in price against the hours waiting in line.

When I turned fourteen he didn't have to make that choice anymore. He'd send me while he continued combining and doing chores.

In the middle of wheat harvest, the mill was open 24 hours a day. It wasn't unusual to pull into the long drive that wound past the lumber company and storage silos and find 20 to 30 trucks in the line ahead. Farmers who lived nearby brought their wheat in wagons pulled by a tractor. The mill was equipped to only unload one truck or wagon at a time. That made for some long waits to unload.

Some farmers chose to take their wheat, after finishing chores late in the evening. Dad would usually send me as soon as the truck was full in late afternoon. Not only did I love to drive the heavily loaded truck, but I got out of doing evening chores too.

Dad trusted a boy of fourteen with the heavy trucks because he knew I was cautious by nature. I was not a chance-taker—even on a dare. Whatever instructions Dad gave me about how long it would take to stop the truck, loaded like it was, I was always sure he'd end with "Make sure to use your head for more than holding your cap on." That was his standard advice, no matter the situation; if I just used my head I'd be all right.

Looking back, putting the responsibility for my actions on my own shoulders was good advice in the 50s and still is today.

Mom would fix me a sandwich and usually a few cookies. Some water in a quart mason jar and I was ready. I'd put the big truck in creeper gear to get started. It was kind of like moving in slow motion. The truck gently swayed though the now-dry dips in the drive that filled with water each rain. Out onto the gravel road and I was on my way. Traffic wasn't an issue. It was unusual to meet anyone until I reached the three-lane pavement that was then U.S. 12, which connected Detroit and Chicago. The tires sang from all the weight as I picked up speed on the pavement. I never got over 40 miles per hour, as Dad's warning about the distance required to stop echoed in my mind. No power steering, no power brakes, but the low-geared trucks back then had more than ample motor power. In low gear they'd pull anything.

I liked driving through downtown Chelsea. It had two red lights. I'd only use first and second gear as I slowly made my way down Main Street. On the far side of Chelsea was my destination. Chelsea Milling Company had been in business for years. They manufactured the Jiffy Mix that became so popular in the '60s.

I'd take my place at the end of the line and soon trucks

and wagons filled the space behind me. We'd moved forward at different intervals. Some only drove pickups which were unloaded quickly.

When you got to within four or five trucks from the unloading gates, a man would come with a small brass container to get a sample of your wheat for moisture content testing. Most followed the man back to the office and watched their wheat being tested. As I remember, 14% was as high as they'd accept. 10 or 12 % was good and the lower the better.

I don't recall there were any dryers for the grain like we have now. Your wheat was either low enough or you took it back home and spread it out on the barn floor to dry. Dad's test in the fields was simple—a few kernels between the teeth and he could tell.

On more than one occasion however, he combined even when he knew the moisture was still a bit high. Those occasions were when the weather threatened to turn bad and he wanted to finish. I knew that meant evenings on the barn floor after dark, with shovels, turning the wheat to get air to the bottom kernels.

I'd get nervous as my turn to pull the heavy truck up on the metal hoist drew near. You needed to be perfectly straight and centered. You also needed just the right speed for the front wheels to climb over the metal plates and drop into the center of the lift. A little too slow and the lift would slide on the cement ahead of the wheels. Too fast and you were likely to bounce over the center and end up with the lift under the cab.

The situation was worse for a young boy like me, since several farmers and some mill workers would all be watching. The lift was mounted on two long overhead tracks so it could move forward or back to accommodate everything from pickups to the longest flatbed trucks.

Yes, I did goof up a couple of times. I never bounded on over, but a couple times I slid the lift ahead and had to back up and try again.

Once the front wheels were off the ground, a man would signal if you needed to inch forward or back a bit so you'd be centered over the huge grate. Then you'd shut off the motor, leave it in low and hurry to lift the center section of the rack so the wheat could flow out.

•

Most farmers built their own grain racks, whether it was on a wagon or truck. To compensate for the imperfections where the wheat might spill out on the ground during the trip to the mill, grain bags were used liberally. They'd be in the corners, along the bottom etc. Even new pickups had enough space around the tailgate for wheat to spill out.

As I lifted the center rack, I had to catch the bags we'd used to cover the cracks. Higher and higher they'd lift the front of the truck. When it was almost empty, I'd raise the two outside back racks an inch or two to get that wheat stuck in the corners.

We all had to give the mill an empty bag for the cleanings from our wheat. After they let the truck down, you'd pull ahead and wait a few minutes. Soon a mill hand would come out and toss your bag of cleaning into your truck. Some farmers required more than one bag.

As I've stated before, my Dad and Granddad were fussy. We'd usually only get half a bag from the over 200 bushels the truck held. The cleanings were destined for the chickens and would last several weeks.

Each farmer received a slip noting the bushels and moisture content of his wheat. When we were done harvesting they would send a check in the mail for our total.

I'd drive home long after dark. I knew Mom would be awake until I pulled the truck into the shed and came inside. Harry had delivered the wheat safety to the mill. I went to bed content that tomorrow, weather permitting, I'd get to do it all over again.

Carl, Geo Jr., Harry, cousin Earl and the 1½ ton stake truck

Hauling milk cans to the creamery

I've mentioned many times in my farm stories about how neighbors helped each other. In the 1940s, that era was in full swing.

Most every farmer milked a few cows back then; it was the steady income farmers depended on for operating cash throughout the year.

Each farmer's cows produced only a few ten-gallon milk cans full a day. The milk needed to be taken to the creamery daily. That meant precious time from other farm chores was taken up driving to Ann Arbor, our nearest market.

Dad joined with our two closest neighbors, Edgar Jedele and Al Hack who also had small dairy herds. Each would take their turn hauling the three farmers' milk seven days a week. Edgar and Al had pickup trucks. Dad had only a ton-and-a-half Dodge stake truck. He built a covered area in the front to haul the milk cans. Al and Edgar had covers that fit over the pickup bed to keep the milk cooler during the summer temps. Each farmer painted his initials and a number on each can and lid for easy identification when the cans were unloaded and dumped.

In the years before, we used a two-wheeled milk cart to pull the cans by hand to the well house some 100 yards away. The cart hauled four cans. The tracks those two narrow iron wheels left across the grass remained visible for several years after we had built a new milk house attached to the barn. The old milk cart now sits by the driveway of one of the grandchildren.

Our milk cooler sat in the well house back then, in front of the cement water storage tank. A windmill kept the big storage tank filled with fresh well water. It supplied the house as well as the four main barns where we kept the livestock. The cooler was electric and was partly filled with water.

A wood step in front of the cooler helped us get the heavy milk cans in and out. I was a teenager before I was strong enough to put the cans in myself. I can remember, as they settled down into the cold water, the cans would get lighter as the weight equaled out. A half-filled can had to be wedged between full ones to keep it from floating up enough to tip over.

If it were Dad's week to haul milk, he'd leave right after breakfast. The morning milk had an hour or so to cool down before he loaded up and headed to Al and Edgar's. The stake truck bed was considerably higher than a pickup, so getting the milk cans up and in was harder. Dad was not big, about five feet, eight inches, but he was strong; I still marveled at his strength when he was in his 80s.

At the creamery the cans were set off on a dock. Each farmer's milk was weighed and a sample taken of the butterfat content; the higher the butterfat, the better price the farmer received. Twice a month the creamery would send each farmer a check for his milk. The milk cans were then turned upside down and hot steam rinsed them clean, ready to be filled again. Dad would load them back in and drop off Al's and Edgar's before returning home.

My first morning job after breakfast, while Dad was gone, was washing the strainer and milking machines. They had to be taken apart and washed in hot, soapy water once a day. After the evening milking, Dad would just run clean water through them and they were ready for morning.

•

What prompted my thought about this part of farming when I was young was remembering the snow-drifted roads that had to be cleared so the milk could be delivered. Here in the winter of 2003, where snowplows and salt trucks spring into action at the first sign of snow, it seems a sharp contrast to the 1940s. We didn't live that far from Ann Arbor—at least in miles— –still, we couldn't count on the county snowplows to clear our road right away. Sometimes three or four days passed before the big trucks with tire chains, their box loaded with sand and gravel, would come plowing down our dirt road.

Along with the neighborly helpfulness, a can-do attitude was prevalent among the rural people I grew up with. It never occurred to anyone to call the county and complain or to sit and hope for the best. They simply got out their scoop shovels and dug their way through the drifts. Dad usually took the milk when it drifted, since his big dual-wheeled stake truck with its weight and height did the best getting through the snow.

He had a set of chains that fit across both dual wheels if he needed extra traction. I can still picture the four of us shoveling through the worst drifts. We'd shovel ahead a ways, then Dad would get a running start and push his way through the partly cleared snow. Then we'd do it again. It was about three miles from our farm to Jackson Road, which was paved and clear. It was called U.S.12 at the time and was a main road to Chicago. Luckily, Al and Edgar's farms were on the way. Dad would stop and load their milk. Each can weighed 100 pounds and made getting through the snow that much easier.

Even after Dad had gotten back home after delivering the milk, our road was still not passable by car. In Michigan the wind usually kept the snow blowing into drifts days after it stopped snowing.

That can-do attitude has stuck with me and I've tried to pass it on to my children. That—and the willingness of neighbors to help one another—are some of my fondest memories of the place and era I grew up in. As I like to remind my son, there's no such word as "can't".

Dad cultivating corn with horses - mid 1990's

Lassie and Pepper

Pepper:
The farm misfit

[To be read as children's story]

I guess every boy growing up wants a dog. This story is about a very special dog. On the farm, dogs are as much a part of life as cows, pigs or sheep. This was especially true back in the 1940s when I was a kid. It wouldn't be a farm without one or two or maybe even an entire family of dogs. They help herd stock, warn when strangers drive in and, in general, take charge to see that everyone and everything is ok. Families like ours, living far from town, depended very much on a trusted dog.

Our first farm dog was called Lassie. She was a big dog, part collie and part shepherd. She was a family dog, protecting and loving every one of us. I later had a dog of my very own. His name was Rover. He was a black and tan coon dog, but that's another story.

This story is about a farm misfit. His name was Pepper. Yes, he was a dog, but certainly not a farm dog. My father, in a moment of weakness, I guess, purchased Pepper at a county fair. I remember he cost $50. Boy, that was a lot of money back then. I remember Mom was a little upset that Dad had spent so much on such a little dog. He was just a puppy then and would fit in the palm of Dad's hand. He had very short hair, brown and white and spotted. His tail had been docked at birth, so it was only about a half-inch long. Well, all us kids took one look and decided, yes, he was cute and adorable, but such a puny thing would definitely not survive on a farm with all those large cows and horses. Full grown, Pepper would still fit into the big side pocket of my winter jacket. We all decided that the only safe thing would be to have Pepper for a house pet. We would keep him inside and just let him out to play. Ah, but Pepper had other ideas!

Officially, Pepper was a toy fox terrier, about the size of a squirrel with long legs. We even had registration papers to prove it. The problem was—Pepper thought he was a 250-pound bulldog. I guess he never looked in a mirror to see how small he really was. As for keeping Pepper in the house where he was safe, well, forget it. Pepper shot out of the house every chance he got. He went right up to Lassie. I didn't understand the conversation, of course, but Pepper obviously told Lassie that he was now taking charge. Of course, he seemed to be assuring Lassie that she could still help. Well, ok, they would *share* the duties of protecting this family and herding the farm animals. Lassie looked at us with eyes that seemed to say, "What did I do to deserve this!?" Lassie, bless her heart, was very patient and accepted Pepper as part of the family. But I could tell she was as skeptical as the rest of us.

Our attempts to keep little Pepper safe in the house met with complete failure. He started following us to the barns. He would ZIP past the chickens and send them squawking for the hen house. He would walk right up to the pigs and cows, completely unafraid. He seemed determined to show us all that he was A FARM DOG TOO! He always seemed to make sure we were watching. He would walk right up to one of the big workhorses, then stop and look to make sure we saw him. Then he would proudly trot off to find another animal.

About two weeks after we got Pepper, he received his first and only injury. Boy, it scared us kids to death. This is how that fateful day started: Every morning, after milking the cows, we would herd them to a big pasture. They would spend the day eating grass. Lassie was always right there to help. She occasionally had to help round up a cow that would stray and start for the nearby road. We would tell Lassie to fetch. She would run around the cow, nip her heels, if necessary, and bring her back to the herd. Pepper, of course, was right there watching all this. He started going with Lassie on her rounds. We would try to call him back, but Pepper would prance along, pretending he couldn't hear us. But, boy, when we put food in his bowl, he heard that a mile away! Well, on this particular morning, Lassie was out bringing a stray cow in, when another cow headed out too. This was Pepper's big chance! He raced after this huge cow and nipped her heels just like he had seen Lassie do. Ah, but Lassie forgot to warn him that cows can kick. The cow didn't know what happened. She felt the bite but she didn't see Lassie, just this tiny brown and white speck behind her. She let go with a big kick! Pepper flew through the air and landed about ten feet away. We rushed over to him...fearing he was dead. Pepper just lay there. We gently picked him up and discovered he had two long cuts on his belly where the cow's hooves had caught him. We kids ran, carrying Pepper and crying our eyes out. Dad quickly took Pepper—and all us kids—to the veterinarian. Good old Doc sewed Pepper up, told us to keep him away from the cows and sent him home with us. Pepper sure got a lot of love and attention that day.

With stitches down both sides, Pepper was pretty sore. He seemed content to lie on his soft bed we fixed for him. We all agreed, for sure, Pepper had learned his lesson. He would be afraid to chase cows ever again! WRONG! As soon as he was all healed, Pepper was right back helping nip their heels, but he never got kicked again. Oh, the cows would try, but Pepper was just too fast for them.

It wasn't long before the cows became afraid of Pepper. This made him even more cocky. Knowing the cows were now afraid, Pepper would trot right up behind them, not making a sound. Suddenly, the cows would see him and break into a run with ol' Pepper strutting right along behind. He seemed to be smiling to himself. He was the boss now. We still worried because we knew a big cow could squish Pepper with just one foot. But Pepper never gave that a thought. He was absolutely fearless!

That was the start of many adventures we kids shared with a little dog named Pepper. He lived with us for many years. We kids loved him and he loved us. We knew that Pepper would attack a full-grown lion, if necessary, to protect us. We trusted him completely and he never let us down.

If my dad hadn't purchased him at the county fair that summer day, Pepper would have grown up as somebody's cute little house pet. But, just like us, animals don't know what life has in store for them. Pepper proudly accepted his life with us. He faced the dangers and did more than his share of the hard work and, despite all our doubts, Pepper turned out to be one of the best farm dogs ever.

Alex moved in with the pigs; preferring them over the chickens

Alex and Henry, farm pets

Farm kids get to know animals up close and personal. There is no way to avoid it. Farms like the one I grew up on were very diversified to say the least. There was no such thing in our neighborhood as "specialized farming." We all had cows, horses, sheep, steers, pigs and chickens. At the very least you learned how to care for them all.

I was nine or ten when Henry came along. Each spring we got out the metal brooder, the tiny water dishes and feeders for the much-anticipated arrival of the baby chicks. Dad preferred Plymouth Rocks and Rhode Island Reds. We'd put our order in around the first of the year.

The chicks would arrive with spring weather in flat, square cardboard cartons at the local implement dealers. You could hear the cheeping and pecking and see the little yellow balls of fuzz through the round holes in the big carton. The carton was divided in four quarters at twenty-five chicks per quarter. Dad would get a big square bale of dry wood shavings along with a bag of special feed and we'd head for home.

What a treat it was to gently take the day-old chicks and playing with them beside the warm hood on the fresh sawdust. They needed no urging. They'd begin pecking in the little feeders immediately. The water containers were quart jars with a twist-on basin that, when flipped over, would dispense about a quarter of an inch into the bottom for the thirsty chicks.

You cannot, no matter your mood, suppress a smile when you're watching baby chicks drinking the first few weeks of life. They scurry in and out from under the warm brooder. A window let us watch as they sat quietly in the warmth, their eyelids slowly closing in contentment. Watching them run around on the shavings was like watching miniature bumper cars. They'd speed up and bump into each other, little bursts of energy with no particular direction or destination. If one found something in the shavings, a bunch more would flock around to see what it was. Their rapid and random motion always brought giggles to us kids. It was exuberance for life in its purest form.

Henry arrived as just one of the little yellow balls of fuzz. As he grew it was apparent Mother Nature had played a mean trick on Henry. He was destined to be the "Hunchback" of our small flock. The older he got, the more deformed he seemed to be. It seriously impaired his ability to get around. We all watched out for Henry, putting his food in a little pile off by himself and standing guard as he ate. He simply couldn't compete with the healthy chickens crowding into the big feeder.

I'm not sure if Henry became so tame because he couldn't run or because he sensed that we were watching out for him. Still, it was unique to have a chicken—even a deformed one—who would let itself be petted. Try as I might, I cannot recall what happened to Henry, I believe he was around for only a year at most.

Alex—who I won at the fair by tossing a dime into a small glass plate—was a duck. I was in my early teens by then. Since he was the only duck on our farm and had to be raised by us kids instead of with a mother duck and siblings, no one thought he would survive long, especially Dad.

He was only a few days old when I won him at the fair. He ate the chicken feed without a single complaint. He would follow us almost from the first day. I was soon taking him with me as I did chores.

He'd waddle along behind, keeping a sharp eye for bugs along the way. Occasionally he'd quack loudly and go running by me. It was always for the same reason. I'd turn and, sure enough, one of the big farm cats would be stalking him. It almost seemed as if Alex knew the predicament he was in, was aware of the slim odds for his survival. He was determined to overcome them and survive he did. There were several close calls, not only from the cats, but the hooves of the other farm animals. Alex learned to be alert and nimble to avoid being stepped on.

He grew quickly and, boy, what an appetite he had; he was like a vacuum cleaner walking behind me. He scooped up bugs as we walked in an ever-widening path. Once he was too big to be a temptation for the cats, Alex roamed on his own through the grass and weeds. His favorites were crickets. Sometimes, after chores were done, he and I would go around looking for old boards under which crickets like to hide. I'd lift up the board and Alex would instantly scoop in and swallow all the crickets before they could find another hiding spot. As he ate, the pouch, or crop, on the side of his neck would get bigger and bigger. I'd remind him occasionally he was beginning to look like Henry, the deformed chicken.

We had no pond near the barns so Alex made do with the mud puddles, which always lasted a few days after each rain. Unfortunately, Alex was pure white except for his eyes and bill. Not a good choice of color considering the lifestyle he was forced to live.

Alex spent his first winter in the chicken house. He was close to fully grown now and his head towered above the chickens. His habits were a whole lot different to put it mildly. He did not spend his nights up on the roost with the chickens. He'd settle in a corner with his back to the wall. The chickens, I could tell, were aghast at Alex's eating habits. He'd lower his head into the metal feed trough and gulp food by the billfull, only stopping occasionally to wash it down by emersing his bill into the water, creating a cloudy mess in the once clear water. The chickens stood back and just watched, bobbing their heads, turning toward each other, unable to comprehend the vulgar display they were watching. When he'd finished, the chickens would cautiously approach the trough, take a couple of quick pecks at the food, then cast a wary eye toward Alex. It took all their will power I could tell, to put their beaks daintily into the murky water Alex had created.

By the next winter, Alex had decided on his own that the pigs were more his style. He moved his residence to the big hog barn on the side where we kept the feeder pigs. We fed them twice a day. A barrel sat in the alleyway. It held the slop we'd mix once a day. After a brisk stirring with a paddle, we'd dip the mixture of feed and water into the long cement trough.

Upon hearing the paddle hitting the sides of the barrel as we stirred, the pigs would come rushing in, jockeying for a place at the trough. Alex would be right in the middle of them. I'll give him this, Alex could gulp down slop as fast as any pig on the farm. He'd eat his fill, sometimes completely disappearing under the mass of pigs, and then retire to a safe distance as the pigs, blessed with a tongue, licked the trough clean. He ended up with scars on both webbed feet, but that never deterred him from being one of the first in line each time I fed the pigs.

The hog barn had a second advantage for Alex. That first winter he'd sat alone on the cold cement floor in the chicken house. This winter, and all those to come, Alex spent sitting on the back of a pig as it lay sleeping. They had gotten used to Alex by now. He'd walk unpredictably across the backs of several pigs as they lay resting before settling on one for the night.

For all practical purposes, Alex was now a pig. He never once went back to those persnickety chickens.

We always took some of our farm animals to the Chelsea Fair. The pigs, mostly mine, were registered Durocs. Alex had taken up with Curly, the big boar, as his permanent residence. As we loaded Curly for the fair, Alex ran up the chute and into the truck too.

Since Dad made no objections, we decided to let Alex stay with his favorite pig. He created quite a stir among the many people coming through the tent as he sat proudly atop a sleeping 700-pound pig named Curly.

A few years later we were phasing out of the hog business. Cows and the milk they produced were more to our liking. We had all registered Holsteins and were getting quite a reputation on the show circuit for having winning animals. We sold the last of the pigs and plowed up all the hog lots to plant crops.

What to do with Alex? An uncle, who occasionally visited, had ducks and chickens on his small retirement farm. He wanted Alex, so we gave him to the uncle who promised not to ever eat Alex for Sunday dinner.

I never saw Alex again, but used to get periodic reports that he was doing well. I felt bad even though Alex had a good home. I knew it was rough for him to have to put up with those darn persnickety chickens the rest of his life. I hope he at least found a lady friend among the ducks.

Myrtle with twin calves

Myrtle

Like all of our registered Holsteins back in the 1950s, Myrtle had a three- or four-word official name. I don't recall what it was, but each one of our animals had a certificate, as fancy as any humans. It had a green scrolled border and an embossed stamp of authenticity.

I do recall she was born in Canada. Dad had purchased her at a monthly auction up at Williamston, Michigan. A great many of our herd came to us this same way.

We were milking between 25 and 30 cows at that time. We had two Hinman milking machines. They sat on the bedding beside the cow and the long black hose plugged into the vacuum line that ran down the top of the stanchions. A turn of the pet-cock and the milker would start its alternating, pulsating action. The bucket held 60 lbs. of milk and some of the cows would almost fill it.

The metal stanchions were located in the basement of the tall barns, with stone walls around all four sides. Cement floors and large wood beams held the floor above. They were flattened on one side only so the part we viewed as we did chores and milked was rounded the exact shape of the trees when they were felled. A whitewash was sprayed over the entire basement, walls and all, to accommodate the state milk inspectors who visited once a year.

Like all kids who grew up around animals, I quickly learned they all have individual traits and personalities. As the cows stood eating their grain and corn silage, we would start the milking. Those cows who leaked milk as they stood waiting were first in line. Some would wet the floor beneath their hind legs as milk dripped and ran from all four teats. Some would not leak a single drop. Some liked to be milked. They would step and sway gently as the four teat cups were placed and the milk would gush down the clean plastic tube into the metal bucket. Some cows only tolerated milking because they had to. Dairy cows have been selectively bred for many generations to produce much more milk that their newborn calf could consume. They're trained the first time they give birth, usually two years of age, to at least tolerate the milking machine as it takes the place of the nursing calf.

Dad had been raised in an era before they milking machine was invented. He could sit down on a stool and milk a cow almost as fast as the machine. He would still milk cows occasionally by hand, usually the first week after they gave birth. Their udders would be sore and swollen. Since the newborn calf would nurse on only one teat usually, Dad would set his stool down beside the new mother and milk the remaining quarters by hand.

Some liked the hand milking; some didn't, but Dad had a no-nonsense policy. It wasn't a matter of like or dislike, only what had to be done. The cows were required to stand and be milked, like or not.

Cows would reach their peak of milk production within a few weeks of giving birth. The next four or five months, the milk would flow in great quantities. Then they would begin to taper off as they were impregnated to calf again at 12 to 14 months. Each cow was allowed a "dry period" where she was not milked as she prepared to give birth again. It was a brief rest period in a lifetime of milk production that usually totaled over 100,000 pounds.

Dad, if he were still here, would probably remember the circumstance surrounding our discovery that Myrtle preferred to be milked by hand —so much so that she would quickly dry up if milked by a machine.

Records were kept of each cows milk production. This aids in the breeding program for future generations and also quickly tells a farmer which cows are the most profitable. Myrtle had a great production record to this point. It was one thing Dad always checked before purchasing a cow. Here she was, already quickly drying up when she should have been at peak production. I have a hunch that Dad had milked Myrtle by hand for a week or more after she gave birth and she decided she preferred that "hands on" contact to the rubber inflations that slipped over her teats from the milking machine. At any rate, one thing was certain: at the rate her milk production was falling, she would be the least profitable of all our cows and certainly slated for sale and a one-way ride to the stockyard. McDonalds hadn't been invented yet, but people still ate meat!

It was probably no more than a "hunch" Dad had from a lifetime of milking cows, but he got out his stool one night and started milking Myrtle by hand. Within a couple of weeks she was producing over a 100 pounds a day.

She wasn't a very big cow, and Dad had powerful hands. Old Myrtle would stand there, having stopped eating when Dad sat down beside her. She'd half close her eyes as if in a trance while the rhythm of two big streams of milk hitting the bucket filled the air. I'd watch her back as Dad milked. She was literally bouncing up and down as Dad pulled and squeezed those teats. He'd fill one foamy bucket, empty it and fill another partly full before that udder was emptied.

A few times I had to fill in and milk Myrtle if Dad were in the field combining or maybe a meeting had kept him from chores. It took me at least three times as long and Myrtle would keep turning her head and looking at me. I could tell what she was thinking, but I was doing my best.

Each year as Myrtle prepared to have another calf, Dad would swear he was not going to milk her by hand again that year. He'd start with the milking machine, but Myrtle always won out in the end. He milked her by hand right up till the day she died.

As she aged, Myrtle became crippled with arthritis. She was forced to kind of shuffle along, her hind legs refusing more and more to bend. We put her in a box stall by herself so she wouldn't get shoved and injured by the other cows. Dad would carry the milk bucket to the barn she was in and milk her there. She didn't need to be in a stall. Wherever she happened to be standing, when Dad arrived, pail in hand, he milked her right on the spot. She wouldn't move a muscle till he was finished.

Dad would mention occasionally that he shouldn't have her bred back and calf any more. She was too crippled and old, but Myrtle was still one of our top producers. She got so crippled finally that in the summer we left her stall open so she could go outside any time. There was no fenced yard near that barn, so Myrtle was actually coming out and grazing on our lawn. We didn't worry she'd leave. Some days she only managed to move

15 or 20 feet. We kept her watered and fed grain, but she got skinner and smaller each year it seemed.

I remember it was summer. Myrtle would stay in the yard day and night. We'd set water out for her and bring her grain in a bucket as it seemed too painful to force her to walk back into the barn to eat.

Next to the barn that Myrtle' stall was in was a smaller barn that we ground feed in. It was two stories like the cow barn and had a ramp going up to the floor where the big red feed grinder sat. We had cattle below the grinder. They ran in and out loose. A trap door was near the grinder where we dropped feed to a manger below twice a day.

Summer days for farmers are spent in the fields. That's where we were that day. As crippled as Myrtle was, we never expected her to make her way up the ramp and into the barn floor beside the feed grinder, but that is exactly what she did.

We found her when we came to do chores in late afternoon. She had fallen through the open trap door to the manger below.

There was a family of sad faces doing chores that night. When you're a farmer, you face the reality of life. Animals live but a short time. You try not to get too attached, so many come and go.

Myrtle, was special, one of a kind. Dad had put up with milking her by hand for many years. Most farmers would have sold her years before.

Looking back, I realize that Dad and Myrtle were a lot alike. Maybe that's what created the bond between them. When either made up their mind, there was no changing it.

I don't believe that Myrtle won her and Dad's little mental tug-of-war. It was mutual admiration and respect, a draw. I think Dad enjoyed the singing rhythm of those streams of milk as much as Myrtle loved that personal attention.

Dad and the yellow-jackets

Farmers in the '40s and '50s waged serious war on weeds and thistles. The only farm tools connected to this story are a corn knife and an old fashioned scythe with the curved handle.

No one used sprays. The yellow mustard plants were pulled by hand each spring when they blossomed. Their small, bright yellow flowers made them easy targets as we spread out on foot across each field. My dad was fussier than most that we keep unwanted weeds to a minimum. Let them go to seed, he'd point out, and we'd have ten times as many the next year.

Others on the top-ten list were burdocks and thistles. We had two kinds of the prickly intruders: Canadian and Bull Thistles.

Most of the pulling and cutting fell on the shoulders of us kids. It was the perfect after-school job before chore time or on rainy weekends when we couldn't do field work. With 210 acres, about 2/3 of which was tillable, that was a formable challenge.

Dad felt weed control was a safe job for us kids. Just use care with the sharp corn knifes and make sure to keep a distance from each other when cutting weeds. That was all well and good, but we kids had to face something-far worse, bumblebees! They loved the yellow mustard blossoms and the big red Bull Thistle ones as well. The mustard required a hands-on solution. Bend over the big plants, grasp both hands close to the dirt and pull. We needed to get the roots and all. We'd shake off as much loose dirt as possible, then carry the wilting plant to the fence row and leave it to dry.

Bees don't like to be hurried when they're hard at work, we kids quickly discovered. As I point out in the story about the one who got inside my bib overalls, bees also have absolutely no sense of humor whatsoever. I guess it would be called an occupational hazard today.

On the subject of bee stings, Dad had no sympathy at all. Ignore them, he'd say. Don't bother them and they won't bother you.

Watching him pull mustard while the bees swarmed around seemed to bear out his words. He never got stung.

Still, for us kids who were far shorter and thus eyeball-to-eyeball with the buzzing little critters, they seemed much more intimidating. I'd check out each mustard or thistle as I approached. The thistles I could sneak up on and give a quick whack with the corn knife and they'd fall as I backed to a few feet away. The bees would simply move on to the next one. The mustard was a different story. I'd wait until I had a chance between bee visits and quickly yank them out. I'd carry them, blossom down, so the bees wouldn't find them again until I'd dropped them by the fencerow. Even with my caution, I'd been chased a few times. As spring turned to summer, thistles and burdocks became the only targets.

My biggest fear, by far, was my corn knife blade chopping through a big Bull Thistle and hitting a bee mansion hidden below it in the grass. That had happened a couple of times, the sound of the blade slicing that big thistle at ground level was followed quickly by the dreaded sound of angry bees. It was no time for foolish bravado. Just drop the corn knife and run like hell. Dad had witnessed such an event once and only laughed as I cautiously tried to retrieve my corn knife.

It was a summer morning; rain had delayed any field-work. Our cow pasture lay right behind the barn. There were patches of Canadian Thistles here and there across the field; an occasional Bull Thistle also dotted the landscape. Dad announced he and I would spend an hour or so getting rid of those thistles while things dried out. Dad took the scythe, which required much stronger arms than mine at the time. I was to get the Bull Thistles while he cut those patches of Canadian ones. We went to work each silently doing this job. I'd gotten quite a distance from Dad as I pursued the lone, tall Bull Thistles. I turned to see how Dad was doing. He waded into a big patch of thistles, his long blade slicing wide rows in the prickly mass.

Suddenly he stopped. I saw him take off his cap and swat at something. I couldn't see what it was from where I stood. He swatted again and again, faster and faster the cap flew. Then he dropped the scythe and started to run, continuing to swat the air with his cap. I stood transfixed.

For a man who never ran anywhere, I observed that Dad was doing pretty well. His flight was short lived however. He hadn't gone more than fifty feet when down he went. His head start on the yellow-jackets, which were in hot pursuit, was gone.

I stood where I was, not brave or fool hardy enough to go to his rescue. In an instant he was back up and running again.

He'd gone a quarter of the way across the field before the nest of the yellow jackets abandoned their intent on getting revenge.

Dad dusted himself off then headed my way. " Nest of yellow-jackets," he said in the way of explanation when he got close. I only nodded, not knowing what to say at this turn of events. I had more sense than to mention his advice to us kids or to laugh, however. He'd been stung several times but, true to his image, we went quietly back to cutting thistles until we'd finished. Except for that one patch that harbored the yellow-jackets.

It wasn't until years later when I was a young man that I could share that story to the delight and laughter of the rest of the family. Even Dad had to laugh at the memory.

On the plus side, I don't remember him ever again giving us kids his speech about how harmless bees were.

Dad with his Gibson guitar

4-H in the '50s
(the coins in the sawdust)

The old Ann Arbor Fairgrounds was located near the intersection of Stadium and Jackson Roads on the west side of Ann Arbor. It was where the 4-H Fair was held before the new facilities were built on Saline-Ann Arbor Road near Pleasant Lake Road. There were several wooden buildings housing dairy, sheep, swine, horses, rabbits and poultry. The first building as you entered the fairgrounds was where the projects such as photography, cooking and sewing were displayed. It also housed the only food booth to serve the yearly 4-H participants. This early "food court" was run by the same family every year.

The only 4-H official I can remember from that era is Don Johnson. He later became the County Agricultural Agent. He was a soft-spoken man who smoked a pipe.

We Macomber kids mostly showed dairy cattle. Dad was starting to build a herd of registered Holsteins. We'd each get to pick a heifer calf when we started in 4-H. We had to train them to lead—which was always an adventure.

Being busy seven days a week, as farmers and their kids are, always resulted in a crash course of training for our heifers that last week before the fair. It was always good for lots of laughs as those unruly, frisky animals were taught to walk slowly and stop on command for the judges' assessment. We'd keep that same calf as she matured into a milking cow and had offspring of her own.

Our farm truly was a family operation. Each of us kids was slowly building registered herds of our own. I later added pigs and photography to my 4-H projects.

My dad and mom, George and Mabel Macomber, became the leaders of our club soon after I became eligible to join. My two older sisters were already members. Our club was called the Scio & Lodi Jr. Farmers. There were many fine farm families in our club. We were noted for not only showing quality animals, but were always there for needed improvements to the facilities or cleaning up after the Fair ended. Some names I'm sure still farm in the area. The Freys, Gradens, Webers, Eschelbachs and Duibles to name a few.

One of my earliest memories was at one of those after-fair cleanups at the old fairgrounds. Our family and some others from our club showed up with trucks, forks, shovels, rakes and brooms the day after the fair ended. Each club was supposed to be responsible for the area in each barn they had occupied. The turnout was disappointing to say the least. Only a couple of clubs even showed up. This led to the enactment the next year of a new rule that the premiums a club earned at the shows would be forfeited if the club did not participate in the cleanup. Anyway, Don Johnson was upset.

Our club members quickly cleaned our areas, and then started cleaning others'. We pitched the manure, straw and hay onto trucks and hauled it to a nearby farm and pitched it all back off by hand. We worked barn-by-barn until all that was left was the exhibit building where the food booth had been. All that needed to be done in this barn that had housed the photography, cooking and sewing, was some sweeping and raking the aisles.

All around the counter where the food booth had been was about three inches of sawdust. It had been put there because water from a storm had run in and collected there. We started raking the paper and trash mixed in with the sawdust. To our amazement, coins started to appear. We kids were soon on our hands and knees in the now dry sawdust searching for coins. It was a treasure trove. I've no idea the total amount of coins retrieved that day, but we few kids who had worked all day felt a lot better being the only ones who had showed up. Obviously, as people dropped coins, they had quickly disappeared into the deep sawdust. Since there were usually lines waiting for food, it was impossible to get down and search, so people had just left them.

Over the next several years in the 1950s, the competition for top 4-H club display got pretty intense. Our club made all our own gates and signs. The colors were green and white. I had gotten a jig saw for Christmas so it fell on me to cut letters for all the kids' names and the larger club signs. We got a production line going at the farm. Someone traced the letters on plywood, someone cutting them out, usually me, and someone dipping them in white paint and hanging them up to drip dry. Whether it was our dairy, sheep, pigs or horse display, our exhibit stood out and we won many awards.

Several years after the 4-H fair had moved to its present location, a neighbor, Paul Wild, had won the bid to tear down some buildings at the old fairgrounds. I was in my late teens and he hired me to help. We dismantled them board-by-board to reuse the lumber.

I'm happy that 4-H is still alive and well here in the new century. There were a few people back in the late '50s who questioned the value of the entire program prompting me to write a letter to the editor of the *Ann Arbor News* in its defense. I enclose the criticism and my response:

Taken from the *Ann Arbor News* in the spring of 1975. It was written in response to County Commissioner Raymond Shoultz who questioned cutting 4-H premiums to "affluent farm kids".
Open letter to Comsr. Raymond Shoultz:

What "Affluent Farm Kids"?

I noticed you were in The News twice last night. I could care less about your concern over time spent by the prosecutor on the Scio Drive-In case, your concern nor the Ann Arbor News' coverage of it doesn't fit my idea of important subjects.

But, as a former 4-H-er and farm kid, I take exception to your remark about affluent farm kids. I'd like the names of those affluent kids. I'd bet you the cost of the survey to find them that the only affluent farm kids in the county live in Ann Arbor and have horses which are boarded and trained by paid professionals.

The price of milk to the farmer, for instance, has dropped over $2 per hundred-weight recently. If you think farmers are affluent, get up some morning at 5 a.m., pitch s---, milk cows, bale hay, shovel grain and do the other 100 things in the average work day, quit at 10 p.m. and do it seven days a week and, to top it off, pay from $2,000 to $5,000 just in property tax for the privilege of working that 98-hour week. I can name you at least two programs funded by tax dollars operated in the county, that have the same amount for a budget and yet help a dozen people or less.

You've been in the city too long. What's keeping you and millions of other people alive is not the A&P, but thousands of family farms that still feed you because they love their life, not because they are becoming rich. You better hope more farm parents encourage their kids through 4-H to continue farming.

While we're on the subject, the farmers in the county get back very little of their tax dollars; the gravel roads are terrible, social services are almost non-existent, police protection amounts to having a vicious dog, and there aren't enough farmers left to vote any changes. The one regret the American farmers have is that they've never been able to produce a food that, when eaten by politicians, would increase their common sense, but it's probably just as well because you'd probably import enough of it from foreign countries to keep the price so low it wouldn't be profitable anyway.

The 4-H program you're so concerned about has done more good for young rural people in the county than all the 100s of thousands of dollars you spend on city social services. It would make more sense to double the $10,000 and work toward getting more city kids into 4-H.

Yes, the prizes are only token, but farmers are getting more and more used to "tokens" in everything from profit to representation.   *-Harry Macomber*

At the 4-H Fair

Harry pantomimes Spike Jones on the 4-H Fairgrounds stage

*Harry with a calf,
Don Johnson in foreground*

*Laying out a gate
for a 4-H project*

4-H preparations

Clipping a calf for the show

Rehearsing for a 4-H play

From the 4-H Website:

In September 2002, National 4-H Council received funding from USDA to implement the "Engaging Youth, Serving Community" project. This program focuses action on some of the priorities that emerged from the National Conversation on Youth Development in the 21st Century. Objectives of the "Engaging Youth, Serving Community" program include:

• Youth in rural areas will gain the skills, experience, and confidence needed to emerge as effective leaders and contributing members of society.

• After-school program staff will develop the competencies and skills to provide holistic, positive youth development opportunities to school-age youth in rural communities.

• Youth and adults in rural communities will improve their abilities to work in partnership to address community needs.

Pilot projects are taking place in 49 states and Guam through their respective land grant institutions, including numerous historically African-American colleges and Native American institutions, to engage youth as partners in addressing community issues, to provide safe and inviting places for youth to experience positive youth development in out-of-school time, and to break down the barriers to participation in community life.

Painting cut-out plywood letters for a 4-H exhibit

The Sears table jigsaw

I don't recall where I saw my first electric table jig saw or what I witnessed being created on it that inspired me to ask Dad for one, but ask I did. I think the jigsaw may have been a Christmas present in my early teens. It was made by Sears and, though it no longer works, I still have it.

On our rural Michigan farm where I grew up was a small building we called the icehouse. It was located only about 40 feet from the main house. It had walls over a foot thick, filled with sawdust. It had indeed been used to store winter ice for summer use.

My grandfather had put electricity inside some years before and converted it to a catch-all storage and work shed. It was the modern 1940s and there was no need to store ice.

Inside the old ice house we stored everything from hickory nuts to crates to hand tools. It had a workbench and one end with a big vice bolted to it. Dad used it to sharpen the mower blades on our International horse-drawn mower, and the sickle bar on our Case combine. The icehouse was a "catch-all" for an endless assortment of bolts, nuts, nails, staples, etc. You name it and it was probably in there if you could find it.

A single light bulb and one electrical outlet provided the electric power. It also had a potbellied stove in the center. With all the sawdust insulation it didn't require much to keep it warm in winter and it was a cool relief in summer. We three boys kept our toy tractors, plows, dump trucks, etc. in the icehouse and there was a handy sand pile right beside it. On the bench near the lone window in the icehouse would be home for my Sears jig saw.

A steady stream of wooden farm animals began to flow from the sharp blade of my jigsaw. Pigs were my specialty. Big pigs, baby pigs and boars and sows emerged from my hand drawn patterns. I also made wooden fence, furrowing pens, gates, etc. I tried to make my miniature farm as realistic as possible. Other toys were now possible as well. Toy pistols and rifles, slingshots; anything a farm boy could use to play with in his "spare" time––which as all farm kids know, was all too short and had to be fit in between all the field work and daily chores. Then there were the nine months of school!

Mom and Dad were leaders of a 4-H club—the Scio-Lodi Junior Farmers. There was a competition between clubs at the yearly county 4-H fair for best display. Someone decided that the names of all the clubs members would look good made out of wooden letters and mounted on a flat board. We got stencils and I started. We had a big club, so it took lots and lots of letters.

The letters were all white, mounted on a green plywood board. It was a family production. I'd cut them out on my jigsaw while my brother and sisters would put little eyehooks in each and dip them in the paint bucket. There were three-inch high letters of the alphabet hanging everywhere on wires. For the name of the club, the letters were bigger. We even painted gates white and green to put at each end of each exhibit, dairy, swine, etc. Yes, we did win our share of awards for our efforts.

Today my woodworking equipment includes a Shop Smith and all the accessories. My table jigsaw now is three or four times as big as the tiny Sears one I started out with. It was the start of a lifetime of creating things from wood, from tables to farm tools for my son.

I still remember fondly the evenings after chores on my stool cutting out all kinds of things on my jigsaw.

Adam holding the 12 gauge, waiting to rob a train (for charity). Harry's gang does this twice a year.

My close encounter with the Sears & Roebuck 12-gauge

I ran up the steps and into the back washroom of our two-story farmhouse. I had pedaled home from school in record time. Yep; there they were: leaning in the corner. I could see the lower stocks of two shotguns, barely visible behind the barn-stained, lower pant legs of my dad's coveralls. One, a pale, weathered gray, had been fashioned from an old barn board. It was all wood except for the nail I used as a trigger. It was almost the same size as the real one beside it with its varnished walnut stock.

This wood imitation of the real thing had been my "hunting" gun for the past three years as I stalked pheasants, rabbits and squirrels with our farm dog, Lassie. We were hunting partners through she was as inept at tracking game as I was in shooting it with make-believe bullets. However, our lack of ability to bring home any game for the table had not tempered our enthusiasm for the hunt in the least. Lassie would thrash, barking through brush and tall, dead fall weeds 'til a startled pheasant or rabbit would burst out in the open. She'd give chase. I'd "pow, pow, pow," until it was out of sight. In a few moments, she'd reappear panting, to receive my praise and a pat on the shoulder for a job well done. Then we'd take up the hunt again, flush with our success, alert for the next encounter.

Today would be different. My hand would reach behind those coveralls, searching, until it felt the cold, smooth steel barrel of the real gun. I had thought about nothing else all day. Either Dad had finally gotten tired of my asking, or perhaps Mom had finally given her nervous ok, but he had declared me "old enough" a week ago to hunt with a real gun. My barely ninety-pound, twelve-year-old excited body had followed him out behind the barn after Sunday dinner. He'd let me hold the Sears & Roebuck, single-shot, 12-gauge as he carried an old rusty bucket out into the cow pasture. Dad silently took the heavy gun from my hands. His thumb pushed the lever and the gun broke open with a loud, resounding click, attesting to its solid construction. He reached into an inner pocket of his bib overalls and pulled out a shiny, yellow shell. Another solid click and the gun was closed, ready for my now increasingly apprehensive hands. I looked up at Dad as I spread my legs to steady myself. I can still see that "showin's better than tellin'" nod he'd given me. I was ready! No unnecessary words of encouragement to delay the moment. It was now or wait another whole year. My small thumb circled the hammer and slowly pulled. It' didn't move.

I applied increasing pressure, desperate to prove I could indeed handle this, the only gun my family owned. I ignored my thumb's painful plea to ease up. Finally that hammer gave, like the loser in an arm wrestling match, and clicked into cocked position.

The thought of the awesome power now just a finger squeeze away sent a shiver through me. I took a deep breath and slowly raised the gun to my shoulder, keeping my finger away from the trigger. The barrel slowly lifted. The small gold sighting BB at the end of the barrel seemed half way to the bucket. I closed one eye, struggling to keep the barrel level. Dad's prior instructions as we'd walked slowly to the pasture moments before replayed through my mind as my finger gingerly found the trigger. The gold BB came to rest on the bucket. I gently squeezed as gravity slowly lowered the barrel. I raised it again and pulled hard this time, as soon as the BB found the bucket. The roar that erupted had echoed across the pasture and into the woods and beyond. Some quick footwork had saved me from an embarrassing encounter with the ground behind me. The concussion had stunned and surprised me. I'd never felt it before, of course, standing safely behind Dad as he'd fired at an airborne squawking rooster pheasant.

"Kinda loud," I'd managed as I struggled to regain my earlier confident composure.

Dad nodded. "Be sure you know what you're aiming at," had been his final words on the subject.

I'd watched as he walked back toward the barn and disappeared around the corner. Only then did my left hand reach and touch the throbbing red bruise spreading across my right shoulder. I looked down at the cause of my pain. Holding it in both hands, tucked up under my arm, I pushed the lever sideways as Dad had done to load the gun moments before. The bright yellow empty casing had shot out; grazing my cheek as it disappeared over my right shoulder. I'd totally forgotten the gun ejected the steel-capped casing with considerable force as it broke open. My aching shoulder reluctantly gave equal quarter to a stinging sensation in my cheek. The excitement of firing a real gun was fading fast. Then I remembered. The bucket! Had I even hit it? I squinted into the mid-day sun. It had rolled into a patch of weeds the cows had shunned as inedible. I ran to pick it up and, to my delight, found it riddled with holes!

Now, here it was a week later. Hunting season was officially open. I had permission to use a real gun! My heart began racing as I reached behind Dad's coveralls and pulled out the 12-gauge. I had an hour or more before chore time and milking, which, with the shorter fall days, occupied me until well after dark. I got up on a chair so I could reach the box of shells perched on a high shelf above the row of coat hooks. I took out two, then two more, then an extra one in case. Who knew what game I might bag or how many? I knew I should take off my school pants and put on my chore ones. Like many farm boys of that era, I only owned two pair. I compromised by making a mental note that I would change the moment I got back from hunting. I quickly and quietly opened and closed the door so as not to alert Mom. She would definitely make me change pants and I'd get a lecture on being careful which would seriously cut into my time to hunt.

Lassie had been lying quietly on the top steps when I'd gotten home. One look at the gun in my hands and she leaped up, eager, circling my legs and barking. I tried in vain to quiet her as I hurried to get started down the farm lane before I was noticed. The house and barns soon disappeared behind the trees. I stopped, took out a bright yellow shell and opened the 12-gauge. The seriousness of being alone with a real loaded gun sank in as the loud closing click echoed in my ears. Even Lassie seemed to sense that something was different.

I'd decided early, as I sat at my desk in our one-room rural school, that I would try to get a squirrel first. It would be much easier to hit a target that occasionally stopped moving to look around. A fast flying pheasant suddenly airborne or a rabbit racing through the brush with Lassie sometimes only yards behind seemed too daunting and hopeless a target.

As we came to each wooden gate in the lane that led into each of the many fenced fields, Lassie would stop and look at me; was this the one we'd try? As I kept walking, she'd watch a while, then reluctantly run and fall into step beside me again; the woods was our destination today. I'd stay near the edge where the trees ended and the cornfield began. The squirrels would be gathering their winter supply of food in anticipation of the long northern winter months. There would be plenty of them scurrying noisily from tree to cornfield and back again. I would surely get at least a couple for the next day's supper.

As soon as we entered the woods, Lassie darted on ahead. In her wake she left a visible trail through the deep bed of dry leaves. The peaceful sound of rustling leaves beneath my feet was soon interrupted by Lassies' excited barking in the distance. I started to run! Then I remembered the power of the real gun I carried and the force trapped in that round yellow shell encased in its chamber. I stopped and looked down at the hammer resting so close to the metal tip of that loaded shell. Would it go off if I tripped and fell? Though I didn't know anyone personally who had been killed or injured by the accidental discharge of their gun while hunting, I had heard the stories. Last year, for instance, in a nearby town, a teenager had lost his hand when his gun fired as he was climbing through an old fence. Growing up on a farm was dangerous for children, at best. Dad and Mom had not raised a chance taker.

I walked as fast as I could, acutely aware now of every potential pitfall and the direction that deadly muzzle pointed. By the time I arrived at the tree, Lassie was sitting, looking up, her panting tongue keeping rhythm with her chest. She gave me a quick glance, wondering, I'm sure, what had taken me so long. My arrival spurred a new round of circling the tree and barking. The tree the squirrel had taken refuge in was a mighty black oak. It was just one of many large trees in our woods—a woods that had not witnessed the destructive blade of a double-bit axe or the teeth of a two-man crosscut saw in many years. We had plenty of wood to cut for home heating in the marshes, fencerows and scattered wood lots on the farm.

I slowly circled the tree, my eyes straining to see the small, brown frame of my prey. I searched the small patches of scattered leaves still clinging to the branches above. Lassie was growing impatient, looking from me to the tree and back again. Her renewed excitement told me the squirrel was moving. She could see what I could not. I backed farther from the massive trunk, my neck starting to remind me it was not designed to look straight up for extended periods of time. Finally, on one of the highest branches in the tree, I saw the flicker of a curled tail. My heart was pounding. As I backed a few steps, I could see his outline now. He turned and cocked his head toward me. I raised the shotgun to my shoulder. I noticed it was easier to hold the heavy gun in this position, pointing almost straight up. I took a practice aim. The tiny gold BB at the end of the barrel seemed almost as large as my prey perched high above me. I brought the gun down and rested my arms a moment.

I had made the right choice in prey all right. He was trapped. I had the real gun in my hands this time. I could shoot when I was ready. Even if I missed, I'd get a second or maybe even a third chance, I reasoned, before he could get to a tree with a hole to escape into. I had witnessed my dad slowly take aim at squirrels before. He never missed, patiently waiting for just the right second when his prey was exposed and still. The small brown body would come falling slowly, softly it seemed, to the bed of leaves below. Dad would call Lassie not to touch it, since her instincts were to grab it and vigorously shake the remaining life out of it. I would retrieve the squirrel from the ground so Dad could examine it. The fewer ruffled spots in the fur where the lead BB's had entered, the better. I'd aim a little in front of his head, I thought to myself, to see if I could bring home a squirrel with only a few pellets hitting their mark, leaving the meat on his body unblemished.

I pulled back the hammer with determined strength. I looked up. The squirrel had turned at the sound of the loud click and now faced me. I raised the gun to my shoulder, slowly, cautiously stepping sideways, intimidated, I guess by the thought of shooting him face to face. The squirrel refused to cooperate. He continued to turn as I slowly circled below him. Seconds ticked by. My neck and arms began to ache. Finally, my arms could no longer hold the heavy 12-gauge in that position. I slowly lowered the barrel. My dilemma slowly sank in. The hammer was cocked! I had to shoot at the squirrel or gamble that my thumb was strong enough to safely un-cock the loaded gun.

To un-cock meant I had to pull the trigger while my already sore thumb held the hammer and slowly eased it down. Could I do it? What if my thumb gave way?

I looked at Lassie as if she might have an answer I hadn't

thought of. She was sitting, panting, worn out from treeing and watching this squirrel I now couldn't shoot. Embarrassment swept over me. All I had to do was raise the gun, pull the trigger and, in less than a second's time, it would be over.

The temporary pain in my shoulder would be forgotten as I proudly carried home my first squirrel. I could keep the tail, show it to the kids at school the next day. I looked back up at the squirrel. Maybe if I back up some more, so it wouldn't be so straight up, it wouldn't seem so intimidating.

I firmly grasped the gun, keeping the barrel pointed away from Lassie. I walked back several steps, turned and looked back up at the squirrel. He hadn't moved, but he seemed farther away than ever. I raised the gun again; Slowly the gold BB found its mark, my finger softly, carefully, circled the trigger. My heart was pounding so loud in my ears, I could no longer hear Lassie circling and barking anew as she anticipated the tiny body falling into her grasp. Would she listen to me like she did Dad, and only sniff the twitching body in the leaves after it fell? Her strong jaws could quickly render the tender meat useless if she ignored me and bit down.

I closed one eye. The black shiny barrel seemed to grow larger as I squinted down its long length. My finger tightened on the trigger. The squirrel, too, was running out of patience as the seconds ticked by. He rose up and slowly moved farther out the narrowing limb. The gold BB followed, my finger beginning to sweat where it circled the trigger. I realized then that communication between my mind and my finger had shut down. My aching muscles in both arms started making their presence felt, slowly going from discomfort to burn.

Suddenly the squirrel reversed direction. He started quickly back down the branch. No use trying to hit him on the move. I lowered the gun, fearing I was on the verge of dropping it if I maintained that position any longer.

I could once again hear Lassie frantically barking as she followed the squirrel down the tree. He took off out across a large limb. Picking up speed, he reached the end and, in one great fluid motion, he became airborne. Time seemed to freeze as I watched, expecting him to come hurtling to the ground with Lassie waiting to pounce before he could recover enough to race for the next tree.

His front feet grasped a small limb from the next tree. It bent down from the weight of his swinging, struggling body. Before I could release my held breath, the squirrel was racing across the limb and disappeared behind the trunk. I stood there staring. Lassie, however, as already circling the new tree with renewed excitement. The squirrel reappeared much higher up. I watched in awe at the speed with which he scaled that tall tree.

His destination was soon apparent—a large nest of leaves near the very top. A few short bursts and he disappeared from view.

Lassie sat down, temporarily exhausted again. She turned, tongue hanging, and looked at me. I could almost see the question in her eyes: what are we going to do now?

I stood there a moment, the still-cocked and loaded 12-gauge in my hands, I had a clear shot at the nest. I knew the BB's would penetrate it easily. The squirrel was not as safe as I'm sure he imagined. I remembered hearing it was illegal to shoot into a nest, even if you saw the squirrel enter it. Still, no one would know. But would he fall down if I shot or just die needlessly in that safe haven high in the tree? That thought did not sit well with my conscience. Killing animals for food was one thing; wasting a life, quite another.

The real problem, however, was the fact that I was holding a cocked 12-gauge shotgun in my hands afraid to shoot, afraid to try disarming it. I had not imagined this scenario during the many days I'd dreamed of and longed for the chance to finally hunt with a real gun. I looked down at the source of my dilemma. There was no sympathy in that cocked hammer, resting so deadly just half an inch from the small pin it would strike, creating the spark that would discharge that lethal load of pellets.

I thought about walking all the way home, very carefully, and letting Dad fire or un-cock it for me. That would surely end my hunting this season and shame me in the process. Then a flash throught hit me. What if I pushed the lever to open the gun? Would the bright yellow loaded shell fly out onto the ground, allowing me to un-cock the hammer safely? I didn't know the answer to that question. The risk of the unknown was too scary. No, I had to fire it or release that hammer slowly, gently. Those were my only options.

I brought the gun slowly to my shoulder. I spread my feet in anticipation of the recoil I'd experienced that one time I'd shot it at the bucket. I turned the barrel toward a distant tree and away from Lassie. My thumb curled around the hammer. I gritted my teeth. My thumb tugged at the unyielding hammer. Harder and harder I pulled. Every muscle in my small body intent now on disarming that gun, the hammer gave, just a fraction, freeing the trigger from its frozen, deadly position. I eased the trigger back, holding onto the hammer for dear life. Slowly, little by little, I eased the hammer forward until it stopped on its own just short of the firing pin. I had done it.

Before I eased my grip on the hammer, though, I tried the trigger once more. It moved freely. My held breath escaped in a rush.

I lowered the gun. I walked over to an old stump and sat down, unmindful of its many sharp hickory nut shells discarded by the squirrels as they'd fed there earlier. Lassie came to put her head on my knee. I reached a suddenly weak arm out and patted her shoulder. "I let you down, ol' girl," I muttered. "We should be taking that squirrel home for supper."

Lassie sat down. She put her paw up on my knee. No judgment here; we were still partners.

I suddenly realized it must be almost chore time. Dad didn't tolerate any excuse for being late for chores and that included hunting. I jumped up, carefully turning the 12-gauge at an angle so the ejecting shell wouldn't hit Lassie or me, I pushed the lever. I retrieved the shell from among the dry leaves and, leaving the gun broke open like Dad always did when he'd finished hunting, Lassie and I started back up the lane toward home. Disappointment in myself eased with each step as I reasoned how my loss was the squirrel's gain. He and I would both enjoy a brand new tomorrow.

Harry with his .38 stallion toy pistols. They are now in a velvet lined case in Adam's bedroom.

Knight School 1946

Attending a
one room school
in the 1940s-50s

The wood desks stood in neat rows, arranged by size to accommodate us kids from kindergarten through eighth grade. A high ceiling above and tall windows on both sides framed our classroom. The blackboard and teacher's desk faced us.

One room school buildings dotted the landscape every few miles in the rural farming area I grew up in. I started school in one of these in 1945.

The first one I attended was on Chelsea-Dexter Road. I believe it still stands today and may be a day care facility. Only one memory from that school where I started kindergarten is still with me here in the summer of 2005. We had to each bring a glass quart jar to make a gift for our mothers that Christmas. I had picked one with intricate designs molded into the glass. It had small squares on all four sides. We were supposed to paint these jars in different colors of our own choosing. I rushed mine, excited to see the end result, and the colors of paint all ran together. It was never considered a work of art or heirloom obviously, since I have no idea what happened to it. I'd tease my mother years later that she had crushed my artistic side by not treasuring that one-time Christmas present. Unfortunately I am still burdened today with that same impatient rush to see the end result of whatever project I start. The upside is I never procrastinate.

My family moved to a farm on Park Road that next

Salem Lutheran School 1950

year. My two older sisters and I started attending Knight school which was located at the corner of Scio Church and Knight Roads. The school on Chelsea-Dexter road was brick. This was a wood frame building. It burned some time in the late '60s I believe, the victim of arson. The site is still there today, but only memories still remain inside its fenced area.

I have several memories from Knight school, not all of them good. There were a couple of what we still call bullies at that school. Our teacher, Mrs. Feldkamp, wasn't always able to keep things under control. Memories of being held by my feet and dropped upside down into a snow bank are among my least favorite.

Probably my worst memory is going on an unsupervised field trip into some nearby woods. Occasionally, on nice spring or fall days, Mrs. Feldkamp would let us go for a long lunch hour. The boys would go one day, the girls the next. I was in first grade. The older boys all carried jack knives. Their idea of enjoying nature turned out to be stabbing every frog or toad they could find. I fervently requested to be allowed to accompany the girls from then on.

Hunting and trapping were common activities for farm kids in that era and I eventually did both. However, I never forgot the senselessness of the killing I'd witnessed on that field trip. I also developed a lifelong contempt for bullies of any type.

In school we concentrated on the three R's: Reading, 'Riting and 'Rithmetic. Sports consisted of games of softball and playing Anti-I-Over with tennis balls over the roof of the school. We had a short morning and afternoon recess and a longer lunch period.

After a couple of years, the Ann Arbor Public Schools system annexed the rural area where we lived and closed all the one-room schools. I was too young to be privy to the discussion my parents had regarding our educational future. I'm sure Dad didn't relish the idea of driving us into Ann Arbor every morning and picking us up every afternoon.

There was no rural bus service. No farmer would want his busy day interrupted that way.

The only close school was Salem Lutheran run by the church. It was about a mile and a quarter away from our farm. My parents had never been members of any church to that point and neither had either of my grandparents. It must have been a major decision in their lives. At any rate, we joined the church and enrolled in the school. After taking instruction, we were all baptized. I was nine or ten by then.

My years at Salem Lutheran School were bully-free. Bible study was just a quiet part of the learning process. No day-long emphasis was put on God. Religion did not creep into the other subjects. We learned our math, science, history, penmanship, etc. just like the public school kids. No one had yet come up with the hypothetical slogan, "What would Jesus do?" used in a self-righteous attempt to gain the moral high ground to judge the actions of others. Our actions were held accountable as one human being to another.

Salem school was bigger. It had three floors though all eight grades still occupied only one room. There was a full basement and a second story auditorium where we held plays and social events like the father-son and mother-daughter banquets. There was a second large classroom but that was used only for Bible study on Sunday mornings before church and meetings of our young peoples' group.

A new world of thought was opened when I discovered National Geographic magazines which were there among others for us to read. Reading was my favorite time. Since we all occupied the same room and reading out loud was done on a regular basis, the teacher, Mr. Schmidt, let us read at whatever level we were capable of. When we would sit around the reading table in back, I usually read with the kids a couple of grade years ahead of me. No one paid any attention to such things back then. No one was "gifted" or "challenged". My sisters won spelling bees, I still don't spell well. I also struggled in math.

We did have some homework, but life was dictated by

Salem School 1954

reality. We were mostly farm kids who did chores every day before coming to school. When we got home from school, we changed back into our "chore clothes" and worked until around eight p.m., stopping only for supper at six. That didn't leave a lot of free time for homework. The good thing was that we had plenty of time for study during the day. One teacher for eight grades meant study time while he was busy with another class.

There were two other boys in my grade. We three made up the entire eighth grade the year we left our one-room school for junior high in Ann Arbor. There were less than thirty kids in the entire school.

We had a large playground area at Salem. Softball was again our main sport and we even played a couple of ball games with church schools in Ann Arbor. We always lost since we had to use all ages of kids to make up enough players. The bigger church schools could play all eighth graders.

We even had sex education of sorts. Mr. Schmidt would keep us older boys in for one or two recesses and briefly explain the proper conduct and respect expected of us as we entered manhood. No discussion about the act itself was necessary since we farm kids had witnessed it all first hand in our domestic animals from dogs to chickens, from sheep to cows. We'd already asked the pertinent questions and gotten pretty straight answers.

Our report cards were simple. We got A's, B's, C's, D's, and E's, or variants thereof like B+ or C-, etc.

How did our "one room" schooling measure up when we got to the big schools in Ann Arbor where we were required to take grades nine through twelve? Very well! We were well prepared in the basics like math, reading, writing, history, science, etc. No catch up was required. For me, personally, required participation in sports was my biggest hurdle.

Those city kids may have needed an hour of serious exercise every day. We farm kids did not.

I was by nature, in today's terms, "athletically challenged". I remember the coach tossing me a basketball, something I had never held in my hands until that moment, and telling me to dribble to the basket and shoot. A video of that sequence, if it existed, would be a hit on the "Funniest Home Videos". Gymnastics and swimming were two other physical disasters I struggled with that first year at Slausson Junior High.

Maybe one of the things that made us stand out a little from our city cousins was our sense of individual responsibility. The teachers sensed that immediately and treated us accordingly. They never had discipline problems with us.

I feel fortunate to have attended those one-room schools and gotten the individual attention we all did. I have witnessed young people, especially here in the south, who are graduating from high school and cannot read and write. Add to that the many who are on prescription drugs and we are handicapping young people for life. Our "bigger is better" mentality in the past fifty years has not led to improved education. I wouldn't want to trade places with kids in today's education system.

Salem Lutheran Church

The family

1941: Dad holding me on the farm I was born at on Pleasant Lake Rd. Mom and sisters Shirley and Barb.

Harry, Barbara, Carl

Back row: Carl, Harry, George Jr., Linda
Front row: George (Dad), Mabel (Mom), Barbara, Shirley

Connie and Topsy, Harry and Dad, in front of sister Shirley's house

Sawmill pictures courtesy of Charles Schaible

Wilbur Schaible's sawmill

In that small German farming community where I was so fortunate to grow up there were all sorts of craftsmen. It was pretty much a self-contained community. From a man who knew how to lay the old cast iron sewer pipe, to the man who repaired windmills, whatever the need, there was someone nearby with the skill to fulfill it. Wilbur Schaible was such a man.

It's right to point out also that nothing was thrown away in that era; it was repaired. From re-soling our shoes to soldering our milk buckets, we got the maximum use out of everything we bought. Plastic had not arrived on the farm scene in the 1940s and 1950s. Added to that was the fact that this generation of farmers had grown up during the Great Depression and had dealt with rationing during World War II. Taking care of what you had and making it last a lifetime was engrained in their character. The environmental destruction we have wrought since becoming a consuming, throwaway society must appall that disappearing generation.

Wilbur's first sawmill was located on Scio Church Road. I don't know the history of who started it or when. All the area farmers used it at one time or another. Rough-cut lumber was always needed on the farm. From gates to mangers to box stalls, farmers were always in need of planks and boards. Most farmers cut logs from their own woods for whatever lumber they needed.

Some, like my dad, had trucks big enough to haul the logs to the sawmill. Others relied on Wilbur to send his two black Ford stake trucks to pick them up. That duty usually fell to his brother Leon. He was younger than Wilbur and quite opposite in nature. Wilbur was careful and cautious, while Leon was a little on the reckless side. It fell on me several times to go with Leon on his trips to pick up loads of logs.

Wilbur Schaible

Leon Schaible

My dad even warned me to stay out of Leon's way. That was good advice and I heeded it. Even driving down the gravel roads, Leon went too fast for my comfort. We'd bounce down the sometimes bumpy, washboard roads, dust flying high in the air behind us. That cab rattled uncontrollably and dust filtered inside as we sped along.

Once at the site of where the logs would lay in a straight line where the farmer had pulled them into a clearing with his tractor, Leon would pull up alongside. Each truck was equipped with a winch on the side with a long cable wound tightly on its drum. The controls were located right behind the cab of the truck. Each truck carried two wood poles that were notched to set on one side of the bed of the truck. The winch cable would be pulled out, stretched over to the opposite side, around the first log and back to the truck. As the cable was pulled in, the log would roll up the two heavy oak poles and onto the truck.

We carried assorted chains and two cant hooks with us. We'd use these to position the log once it was on the truck, starting on the side closest to the winch. We'd put as many on that bottom row as would fit. Then we'd set the two poles up on that level and stack the next row on top.

Occasionally Leon would even put a third tier of logs on as I held my breath. The winch was geared so that it would pull even a big log on to the truck with the truck motor idling. That wasn't, however, fast enough for Leon.

I can still picture him standing beside the truck on one leg, the other stretched into the cab and pushing on the gas pedal.

Before the fire on Scio Church road

The log would come hurtling up the ramp and even occasionally roll clear across, break the wood stakes and fall where Leon was standing. He'd always manage to jump out of the way. He'd grin at me, cuss a little and we'd start over.

Once we had all the truck would hold, we'd run chains over them all and, using a toggle chain, we'd tie them tightly to the bed of the truck.

Occasionally we would haul several long logs that hung quite far over the back of the truck bed. That would make the cab of the truck very light, even bouncing into the air as we drove back to the sawmill. I'd hang on; scared we'd end up in the ditch since we couldn't steer with the wheels off the ground. But, as reckless as Leon was at times, he was also skilled at what he did. Neither of us ever got hurt, though Leon did die of natural causes much younger than he should have.

Wilbur and Leon were both full-time farmers too. The sawmill didn't run every day. In the summer it rarely was used. Wilbur would let logs pile up and then run the sawmill every day for a couple of weeks. He also bought logs and cut them for custom orders from outside our community.

That first sawmill I visited as a kid of eleven or twelve had burned one fall day. Since we were out in the country, barns were lost causes as far as the city fire departments were concerned. By the time the volunteers got to the fire hall and then drove to the fire, it was too late for anything except trying to save some nearby buildings and mopping up. The men working that day had managed to save one tractor, a few small things and Wilbur's records. Dad and I drove over to view the remains like most farmers did in that area. Many stayed to help clean up.

Wilbur's farm was located about three miles away on Pleasant Lake Road. That is where Wilbur built the new sawmill

The new sawmill on Pleasant Lake Road

in the early 1950's. It was bigger and he could cut much longer logs than before. In fact, not long after he opened back up, Herb Diuble was building a new barn. He needed logs forty feet long and still a foot square at the small end. Very few trees were straight enough and large enough to fill that bill. Herb found only one in our woods and had to search many acres of woods to find enough. Those huge logs taxed Wilbur's equipment to the max, but he got them cut.

Like most farmers, Wilbur wore bib overalls and smoked a pipe. He also made hard cider which was a staple for those German farmers. At the sawmill there were jugs of it for us to drink. A corn cob would be the stopper. No cups were used. The jug was passed around and everyone took a swig. I took my turn though I didn't much care for the taste of sharing it with the tobacco chewers in the bunch. I always took a sip, too, due to the politeness and respect that we all shared for each other.

The new building that housed the sawmill was probably 40 feet by 150 feet. That's guessing from memory. The open side was toward the east. Tracks for the carriage that carried the logs as they were cut also ran out the south end for thirty or forty feet. This was to allow for the really long logs that needed to be cut such as those Herb Diuble needed.

There was a ramp leading up to where the carriage sat ready for a new log. We'd use cant hooks to get them rolled up onto the carriage. If it was a normal sized log, Wilbur and I could get it on. Bigger ones needed the help of the men who carried and stacked the lumber after it was cut.

Once a log was rolled onto the iron bars of the carriage, it was locked in place by lowering movable sharp hooks down into the bark of the log. These bars and hooks were about four feet apart. They moved in unison forward and back as the log was sawn into lumber. The carriage was probably about forty feet long. Most of the time we were sawing 8-, 10- and 12-foot logs.

One or two men rode the carriage, turned the log and worked the lever that determined the thickness of the board to be cut. When help was short, one man would ride the carriage alone. He was, as they say, busier than a one-armed paperhanger.

When I started working there as a real job I was sixteen. I was skinny, probably only weighed about 115 lbs. On the plus side, I was quick witted and fast on my feet. Wilbur would motion me to come ride the carriage once we were ready to start. I liked it. I've always liked a challenge and still do. I'd move as fast as I could, trying to guess what the next move would be before Wilbur told me with hand signals.

A tall wood handle controlled the carriage's movement back and forth. Push it one-way and the carriage would take the log into the whirling blade. Pull back and the carriage would roll back to where I would move my lever, bring the log out another one or two inches or whatever width was needed.

Timing was everything. The longer it took to turn the log or position it for the next cut, the longer all the rest of the help stood there and waited. Within an hour that first day that Wilbur put me on the carriage, we had developed a rhythm. The harder Wilbur pulled or pushed the wood lever, the faster the carriage would go. I had to actually spread my legs apart to keep my balance.

On the return trip of the carriage, Wilbur would hold up one or two fingers. That was my cue as to how far to bring the metal lever forward; one inch or two inches.

I'd watch and as soon as the log cleared the blade, I'd rack the lever. Before the carriage even stopped, Wilbur would be pushing the lever forward. The big circular blade would chew into the wood and another finished piece of lumber would fall onto the rollers in front of the men stacking it. In moments, that log was reduced to slab wood and lumber.

Wilbur would stop the empty carriage in front of the next log in line. I had to first reverse my lever and back the log holders back to accommodate the size of the next log. I'd raise the hooks and lock them, grab a cant hook and help Wilbur roll the next log on. Jumping from hook to hook, I fastened the log in place, grab on to my lever again and bring the log out toward the blade until Wilbur stopped me.

He'd eye it briefly. If he didn't like the way it lay for the first cut, I'd have to loosen the locks; we'd turn it, then he'd lock if back down. The first cut usually took about an inch to an inch and a half of bark and wood. We usually made a second pass taking another inch off. This would usually make a board, but it needed to be run through the edger in the back, which would trim the bark off both edges at once so it was a usable board.

The slab of bark was rolled all the way back. It was taken by two older men and cut into short lengths that would fit into a wood furnace. These were tossed out on a large pile where people would bring their trucks and load them.

I can't remember how much Wilbur charged per load, but during winter it disappeared pretty fast.

Back on the carriage it was an endless stream of logs. Still, for as demanding as that job was, I was glad to be doing that rather than loading the heavy planks that rolled down that track fresh from the blade on to a wagon or truck.

As soon as we squared one side of the log we'd turn it so the flat side was down. This gave us a straight flat surface to work with while finishing sawing the log. Once the log was squared on all four sides, Wilbur would usually cut it down the middle. We'd then stack those two on top of each other and cut two boards or planks at once. In order to hold the two halves together so one didn't fall off onto the rollers, Wilbur would stop the carriage and leave maybe an inch of wood holding. He'd slowly back the carriage up, dragging the cut piece along until it cleared the blade and we could flip them.

Wilbur still had a slight German accent. He could speak it well. He was quiet and even tempered which was a good thing because it was easy to get perturbed at the help when everything went wrong. One hazard was sawing into a hidden nail.

Many farmers fastened fence or barbwire to trees if they were in line with a fence they were building. Many years later, when the tree had matured and long ago grown over and hidden the nails & staples deep inside, someone would cut the tree down and bring the log to Wilbur's. Just one staple would dull the blade enough to require stopping and sharpening.

This was costly as men stood around while Wilbur sharpened it. First he would hit each tooth with a steel shaper. He'd lay the shaper over a tooth and hit it with a hammer once or twice. He did this all the way around the blade. They he'd take a flat file and with only his eye as a guide he sharpened each tooth individually. On that big blade—almost as tall as I was—there were a lot of teeth.

Newly sharpened, the blade would actually sing as it

bit into the oak logs. The two John Deere D tractors that powered the blade and carriage would bounce slightly in unison as their throttles opened to accept the challenge of keeping that huge blade spinning at top speed.

When things were going smoothly, it was a beautiful scene to be part of. I'd ride that carriage back and forth as Wilbur moved that lever with a touch that would be the envy of a skilled surgeon. Sometimes he'd light his pipe without missing a beat. He'd crook one elbow around that lever so he could light his pipe with both hands.

We'd get going so fast that occasionally I'd start to move my lever just a fraction of a second too soon and catch the blade before it cleared the log on the return trip. Though it didn't hurt anything, the sound of it always scared me. I didn't want to be the reason for any down time because I broke something.

•

I loved the sound of those two John Deere tractors. My dad had all International or McCormick Deering, which was the forerunner of Farmall.

Two of ours had to be hand cranked to start. On the two-cylinder John Deere's, it was all different. They were started by turning a big flywheel on the side. First you'd open a petcock on both sides to relieve some of the compression so you could turn the flywheel. You'd choke it for a couple of turns. Air would escape out the petcocks as you turned the flywheel. It made a loud swooshing sound.

At sixteen I wasn't really strong enough to turn them over well. Occasionally I'd give it a try and got so I could start them, but it was hard. When they finally fired, the flywheel would take off, spinning out or your hands. You'd close both petcocks and they were ready for work.

Both tractors sat on oak planks. I liked to watch them when we'd saw into a big log. The throttles would open in unison and they literally bounced up and down on those planks. The tires would give as they bounced so they never actually left the ground. For a teenaged boy it was fun to watch.

Speaking of my age, Wilbur told me when he hired me that I was supposed to be eighteen to work at the job on the carriage; I was prepared to lie about my age if it ever came up and Wilbur was inspected. Luckily, that never happened.

•

I hadn't mentioned the sawdust that resulted from that big blade making endless passes through log after log. There was a wide hopper under the blade and a fan that blew the sawdust up a long overhead pipe and onto a pile just outside the building. Farmers, including my dad, brought trucks and hauled the free sawdust home for bedding in the barns. It was great to put in the gutter and on the walks behind the cows.

In the back corner of the building, in addition to the buzz saw and edger, was a planer. It was seldom used but I do recall a couple of times we hooked one of Wilbur's newer John Deere's to it and planed the rough-cut lumber to a smooth surface.

It took a minimum of five to six men to operate the sawmill. Sometimes as many as eight to ten were there if we were going to saw long logs and bigger timbers.

I was driving on my own. At noon we'd stop for an hour for lunch. I'd sit in my car or on a pile of lumber and eat. Wilbur went to the house for his meal. He and his wife had four daughters. The oldest about my age and I remember how nervous I'd get when the two older ones would come out occasionally to watch. Wilbur kept hoping for a son and finally Charles arrived; he was just a baby when I worked there.

In 2005, Charles still lives on the farm and still occasionally saws a little lumber. I was told he uses just one modern tractor now, but it's still a John Deere.

Wilbur was typical of the men I grew up around. Honest, hard working, polite, respectful and, at the same time, an individual in his own right. I remember he usually sat in the back row at church. His deep voice could usually be heard above most of the rest of us. He unashamedly sang his heart out.

•

I've often tried to find the right words to describe that generation of men and women. Tom Brokaw summed his feeling up by calling them The Greatest Generation. The question is why they were the way they were. What created that attitude of personal pride, individual character and a deep sense of common good? We are all shaped by the history being created around us, by our individual interpretation of life's daily turmoil.

I didn't share what shaped that generation, but I have profound respect for what it produced! It wasn't writers or poets that influenced them. They weren't born into America's best times, but somehow they made sure America's best years happened. It's almost as if they individually and collectedly arrived at a set of values that formed a concrete base to build on.

They understood what was needed to build a society they could flourish in and they set about, without words, determined to create it.

My first job for pay... helping the neighbors

My hair was matted with sweat under my cap. Beads of sweat were trickling down my temples as I jumped in the Ford pickup and headed back to the oat field where our neighbors Edgar Jedele and Al Hack were combining.

It was July; I had just turned thirteen. Since my dad was blessed with three sons and my older sister who liked working outside and doing chores, he had "farmed me out" to help the neighbors. Actually, I was working for Edgar. He paid me four dollars per day. That day was from eight a.m. until we'd finished milking at night around eight p.m. I did chores and ate breakfast at home each morning before jumping on my bike and arriving at Al's or Edgar's farm.

Edgar and Al lived across the road from each other. Edgar and his wife Elsie had no children. Al had married a divorcee late in life. She had two teenaged children. Her son had no interest in becoming a farmer, so we seldom saw him. That meant that if you helped either Al or Edgar, you helped both as they did everything together.

They both had combines, Edgar a six-foot Massey Harris and Al a five-foot John Deere. Edgar had an International pickup, Al a Ford. Two combines, two pickups and only one me!

When I got back to the field, the International was sitting loaded, about twenty-five bushel of golden oats gleaming in the bed. There wasn't time to admire and appreciate the beauty of that summer scene. I was determined to keep up with them. I jumped out of the Ford, into the International and headed back to the barn. The flutter of the oat stubble as it rubbed the bottom of the pickup accompanied me until I pulled out onto the gravel road.

Most every farmer cut the oats as high as possible. The ragweed was getting almost as tall as the oats and oat straw is dustier than wheat. That made it less desirable as bedding.

Arriving at the Al's or Edgar's farm, I'd back the pickups up the barn hill and onto the planks of the barn floor, the loose ones creaking under the weight. I'd ease back to the small aluminum elevator and stop. Dad always taught us to think ahead, a habit I still possess. I wasted no motion as I plugged in the elevator, grabbed the scoop shovel and jumped onto the load of oats. In seconds oats and dust were flying up, up, up, into the grain bin. The grasshoppers—dead or with legs missing—and slow moving stinkbugs, joined the flow of oats as I shoveled feverishly.

My shoes were filed with oats after the first load. There wasn't time to take them off after each load. Besides, after a couple of loads, you get used to the feeling your feet are packed into your shoes like dirt around a newly set post. I'd empty them at noon and throw the oats out for the chickens that ran freely in the yard.

Anyone who has ever shoveled oats into a granary bin knows the kind of dust you make. My nostrils would be plugged almost full by the time that last scoop had dropped into the bin. Within minutes I was headed back to the field.

I miss those old fashioned v-shaped windows that swiveled way around to bring a nice breeze into the interior of the cars and trucks back then. I made full use of them as I hurried back to the field, relishing the breeze and fresh air.

On the plus side, Edgar and Al always kept some bottles of pop in the milk cooler just for me, usually a Nesbitt's Orange or 7-Up. I appreciated the fact that they took more "drink breaks" than my dad allowed.

Al and Edgar would have swigs from the brown jug with the corn cob stopper. It was homemade hard cider, a staple in the German farming community I grew up in. I'd tried a swig or two but had to be real thirsty and I never developed a taste for it. They'd share the jug, passing it back and forth. Al didn't seem to mind a bit that Edgar chewed tobacco constantly, nor did Edgar seem concerned at the pipe Al kept in his mouth all day. I reasoned from the taste of the stuff that the hard cider killed any hapless germs it encountered on the way down anyway.

I helped them bale hay earlier that summer, yes they both had balers too. The good part was that Edgar and Al loaded and Al's dad, Ed, and I drove tractor.

The three of us would unload since Ed was in his 80s

and couldn't get up into the mow. Ed had also never quite got the hang of modern farming. He'd been a horseman all his life until now.

When he was driving that John Deere, he looked straight ahead—never looked back. If the baler mis-tied, we could see Al waving and hollering, but to no avail. He'd have to jump off the wagon and run ahead of the tractor to flag Ed down. The humor of the scene didn't escape Edgar and me, as he'd wink and smile at me as we baled along beside them.

I feel privileged to have been the oldest son and the one Dad "farmed out" to help the neighbors. It created a deep respect and appreciation of the differences in us all. Despite our personal habits and quirks, we share the same basic values and needs in life.

That era of farm neighbors helping each other is pretty much gone. Modern machinery is geared to one-man operation from fieldwork to chores. I'm forever grateful to have gotten in on at least the tail end of neighborly-shared threshing, corn husking, silo filling, etc.

Those memories of grown men and boys working shoulder to shoulder are ones I cherish.

6580 Park Road: Edgar Jedele's barns and house today

Across the road: Al Hack's house and drive shed today

The snapping turtle's new home

The tiny mud turtle was only a few feet from the edge of the small pond back in our farthest field. I cautioned my little sister to be quiet and still. I slipped off my shoes and socks, rolled up my pant legs and walked slowly toward the murky water. Turtles were my favorite. This one was about the size of a silver dollar. Maybe I could catch him, though experience told me the chances were slim. He sat watching us from a small stick protruding from the water.

It was a typical Michigan summer day. I don't remember the circumstances, but I was in charge of my little sister, the baby of the family, while Mom and Dad were gone. My two brothers were playing in the big sand pile near the icehouse. My older sisters must have gone with our parents or they'd have been in charge and I would be weeding the garden, cutting thistles or any number of jobs Dad could have found for me. There were no "idle" days on our 210-acre farm in the mid 1950s.

Anytime I got a few 'free" hours, usually on Sunday afternoon, I'd head for the woods or ponds that dotted our farm. I set out this particular morning down the lane with my little sister in tow or riding every so often piggyback style.

I had started high school. She was in kindergarten. I should point out that our farm lane was just shy of a mile in length. Our farm was a long rectangle shape. The lane went down the center, with frequents gate openings to each field along the way. At the end you could go through the left gate and be in the stump lot, the last field cleared years ago, or take the right gate and enter the big woods.

It was there in the stump lot that I cautiously attempted to get close enough to grab that turtle. My feet were tender. We were not allowed to go barefoot and risk injury to our feet. The water, as I ever-so-slowly slipped my foot into it, was warm. I was in slow motion hoping, with a couple more steps, I could snatch that turtle.

With the algae, dead leaves and debris, I could not see the bottom. I was feeling my way now that both feet were in the water. I could never have gotten that close to an older turtle. This one sat so still, my hope was growing. Another step and I could lean forward and ...then he was gone. I put both hands in the water, still hoping to feel that small shell below the surface and pull him up. I inched forward, the water up to mid calf now, the muck squeezing up between my toes with each step. I slowly widened my search area, unwilling to let my sister down as she watched expectantly from the edge.

My next step didn't feel right. There was no mud as I eased my foot down. I had stepped on a rock. It was slimy and slippery and quite large. I backed up a step, bent over and parted the algae. A form slowly took shape: a snapping turtle, about the size of a large wash bucket. By pure luck, I was standing at his rear.

I had encountered snappers before, but always on land as they crossed slowly from one small pond to another. They were fearless. No pulling in the feet and head as I approached. Opening their mouth, instead, as a warning if I got too close. I'd gotten a stick once and tested one to see if he'd really bite. The suddenness and speed of his strike at the stick caused me to drop it and step back. They might crawl real slow, but that head moved like lighting.

As an adult I am known as a cautious, common sense individual. What I did next is proof that it wasn't a born trait, but one I developed through experience. I reached into the water and grabbed the snapper by its tail. I reasoned that, as long as a snapper's neck was, it couldn't reach clear around to its tail. I pulled. That snapper felt like he was embedded in that murky mud.

I used both hands now, as the tail was five or six inches long. Slowly he emerged, head and feet extended. I backed up, half sliding him until I reached shore. The sight of that head and slime-encrusted shell scared my sister. She backed farther away. I let go of the tail. The snapper stayed put, looking around for something to blame for this rude intrusion.

I picked up my sister and brought her close so we could study this holdover from the dinosaur age. Having decided, I guess, that there was no one to stop him, the big snapper started back toward the water. I put my sister a safe distance away and again picked up the snapper by its tail. I carried it at arms length about fifty feet out into the field. I was feeling brave, I guess, or being plain foolhardy. At any rate, I waded out into the pond again. Within a few minutes, taking very cautions steps, my foot encountered another smooth surface. It was another snapper, a bit smaller that the first.

I carried him out beside the other one who was once again steadily making its way back to the pond.

I stood looking at the two snappers. They wouldn't make very good pets for sure. Then I remembered that nature area we were setting up at the new high school in Ann Arbor. It had a fair-sized pond on it. These snappers would be my contribution to its wild life. My dilemma was the distance we'd have to walk back, almost a mile, get something to carry them in and come back. They would be back in the water, hidden in a new location and probably in no mood to be pulled out again.

At the edge of the woods was a pile of old fence posts, brush, broken boards etc. that we would burn come winter. Mixed in were some bundles of baler twine that had been pulled from the straw bales as we bedded the barns. I carried the snappers to the fence and tied their tails to it with some twine.

It was a long walk back to the house. I found a big washtub for the big snapper and a large bucket for the smaller one.

Neither my sisters nor my brothers shared my excitement over the turtles I had found. No one volunteered to walk back with me and retrieve them. I had to take my sister, so I persuaded her it would be a fun trip. I'd pull her in our little red wagon.

After getting a cushion off the tractor seat, we started out. When we finally arrived at the fence, no turtles. The two snappers were gone! The twine still clung to the fence. I ran toward the pond. I spotted two slow moving jagged shells making their way slowly toward the pond. I put them in the buckets.

There was now no room for my sister. She left no doubt that she would not get into the wagon with those snappers even if there were room. She was also not walking back. Carrying her alternately in one arm then the other, we slowly made our way back—all four of us. At least the turtles didn't complain.

My treatment of those two snappers may have seemed cruel to some, but I was as careful not to hurt them as I was of my sister. They did make it alive and well to their new home at the high school pond. At least my fellow students and teacher appreciated my barefoot efforts in bringing them there. We all applauded as they disappeared beneath the water in their new home.

To this day, I still stop and move them when I see a live turtle in the road. They may have survived since the age of dinosaurs, but they have no defenses against a car or truck traveling down the roadway.

Switching from horsepower to tractors in the 1950s

I sometimes regret having been born too late to have been part of the era of horse power. By my early teens, tractors had replaced most of the quiet sounds of horse and harness laboring in the fields.

Field work may have gotten easier and faster for the farmers, but it also got a lot noisier and maybe a little less personal. That close contact with every foot of the farm that had marked several generations slowly gave way to the unforgiving tire treads of ever faster and bigger tractors. Many places in the fields that had been easily accessed by horses were abandoned and left fallow because of the tractor's weight and turning radius. A subtle change in attitude accompanied this rapidly changing farm scene, culminating in the no-till-spraying frenzy wreaking havoc with the land and environment today. One thing that hasn't kept up with this ever faster technology is an assessment of the irreversible damage being done by today's farming practices. It will be left to future generations to deal with the outcome.

Having actually lived at the end of one era and the beginning of another, I still today appreciate and value the quiet of the days before combustion engines roared over the fields. It could honestly be said back then that farmers were truly good stewards of the land.

My earliest memories of doing chores at our farm on Park Road near Ann Arbor, Michigan included cleaning the horse barn. Dad and Grand Dad both kept their teams in the two-story barn. I believe there were eight individual stalls. Teams were kept together whether side-by-side in the fields or in their stalls.

Large wooden pegs lined the walls where the harness for each hung. Planks were on the floor of the stalls to keep the horses' feet off the hard concrete. The sides of the stalls near the horses' heads went all the way to the ceiling. There was a built-in hay manger and a small feed box for the whole oats that were fed. The stalls were wide enough so Dad could walk in carrying the heavy harness and put it over the backs of the horses.

In one corner of the barn was an enclosed oat bin. Next to it was a wood ladder going up into the haymow filled with loose hay.

The horses were seldom pastured back then. They were

either in the field working or standing quietly in their stalls.

I'd walk into the main door and immediately face the rear end of several horses and the piles of manure behind them. We carried most of it out with wide, many-tined manure forks. We then pushed a metal scraper behind them to finish up. Some fresh straw and they were set until evening chores.

The only tractors around were Grandpa's big steel-wheeled monsters that powered the thresher, corn husker, silo filler, etc. Dad also had an old McCormick Deering 10-20 that had been converted from steel wheels to rubber. As a boy of eight or nine, I was not near strong enough to even steer those tractors. They were also hand cranked to get them started.

Horses were losing their place as the main power source for working the fields. Dad never really taught me how to drive a team. For my size and strength it was too dangerous. He did let me hold the reins occasionally, just for fun.

In 1950, the year I turned ten, Grandad had purchased another farm about five miles away on Parker Road. Dad purchased an almost new tractor. It was a small International B-N. It came from the factory with rubber tires, individual brakes and even an electric starter. It ended up doing much of the work formerly done by our teams of horses. It even came with a two-row cultivator that was raised and lowered by hydraulics.

Dad cut the long horse tongues off the sickle mower and side delivery rake so we could pull them with the B-N. Even the job of hauling hay wagons was switched to tractors.

Our next tractor was an International C. It was a little bigger and stronger than the B-N. We even began using the old 10-20 more. None of us kids could yet push in the stiff clutch and shift gears.

I remember hauling the hay wagon around the field while Dad loaded. My sister Shirley and I would sit on the seat together and join forces to push the clutch in and steer. I can still picture us both on the seat, both with one foot on the clutch, holding on to the steering wheel with both hands to keep from sliding back from holding that clutch. We couldn't let go to shift it out of gear, so we stayed, straining until Dad gave us the O.K. to go ahead again. I finally got strong enough to handle the 10-20 alone and loved plowing with it all day long.

Dad kept his horses for many years after the arrival of the B-N. They did less and less work each year. They were pastured a lot and we kids would occasionally ride them down the lane bareback to get the cows up for milking. They were never broke to ride and we had no saddle. We just led them close to a wire fence so we could climb it and slide onto their backs. They leisurely walked wherever we steered them.

Dad finally gave in and sold his last team. I don't remember the year, but it was a sad day. He was about the last farmer around to quit using horses.

Years later, when Dad and my two brothers had moved to a different farm near Manchester, Dad bought a team of Belgian draft horses. He even did some fieldwork with them on occasion. He had saved some of his horse-drawn farm tools and bought a few more at auctions. Dad also started driving in parades and fixed up his old farm wagon, now sporting rubber tires, with extra seats so he could give rides at the annual Manchester Chicken Broil. He did some weddings, delivered Santa at Christmas and became noted for his team and driving skills all over again in the 1980s and '90s.

His last team was a pair of Percherons that a lady had given him because no one ever drove them. They were in their 20s and pure white. Besides driving in parades, he hauled manure, raked hay and sowed wheat with this team. I was lucky enough to get to help him some during his last years. I even got to try my hand at sowing wheat one fall. I quickly realized the skill required to guide those horses in the many tasks they had once done on a daily basis. My respect grew tenfold for these farmers who had relied on horsepower before tractors came along.

As a final tribute to the great horseman Dad was, we used his last team to haul him to his final resting place. He would have been truly honored.

February 2000: Horses pulling Dad's coffin to the cemetery. Driver is Ralph McCalla. Brother Carl is riding with him. Melanie and Harry are walking behind.

Railway trip
a test of who I was

I was upset the first time I discovered it was missing some fifteen years ago. "It" was a diary I had kept of my rail trip to Albuquerque New Mexico back in 1957 when I was only 16 years old. I wasn't a regular passenger back then, sitting in a reclining seat, staring out the window as the countryside flew by. I was riding in a boxcar, one of two filled with young dairy cows headed for a big milk-producing farm in New Mexico.

I had kept a diary almost hour by hour in a small note pad that fit into my shirt pocket. With its loss went many details that have escaped into the recesses of memory, not easily brought back some forty-eight years later.

The trip took place in March. I remember well since winter had not released its hold on the temperature, which hovered in the 30s I had quit school the previous fall after finishing my sophomore year. Having read Ayn Rand's Fountainhead, I was feeling pretty independent, but not sure of my direction in life. I wanted answers to lots of questions running through my mind. Those answers weren't found in the classes I reluctantly sat through. I helped Dad full time on the farm. We also cut firewood and sold it to steady customers almost weekly.

At a dairy cow sale Dad and I attended, the auctioneer, upon hearing I wasn't attending school, inquired if I would be interested in accompanying some heifers to Albuquerque. It would be a four- or five-day trip out and then I would ride a passenger train back home. The auctioneer was CB Smith, a highly regarded dealer in dairy cattle. In my early 20s I would return to his sale barn and work for him full time until deciding to return to school.

CB assured my dad the trip would be easy. I'd have to feed some hay and make sure the water tanks were kept full, but no hard labor was involved. He also told Dad there was no real danger since the train crew would watch out for me. Had I known CB better, I would have taken both statements with a grain of salt. He was such a self-assured man that doubt in his own ability or anyone else's for that matter, never crossed his mind. For CB it was an easy undertaking. He and my dad came from a generation that never said can't. They simply figured out a way, no matter the situation, and then did it—a great attitude to carry through life.

It was spitting snowflakes when Dad dropped me off at

the auction barn in Williamston, Michigan. I had a change of clothes in a box plus extra socks and underwear. CB had some of the workers at the sale barn already planking up the big doors on the rail cars that sat on a siding in Lansing, about twelve miles away. I jumped in his car with my box of clothes and CB sped to the site.

The men were just finishing up. Since CB had shipped cattle this way before, he knew what must be done to assure their safe arrival. By planking the doors of the rail cars, I could open them as we moved south and west and the weather warmed. Two big fifty-gallon drums were in each car. I was to keep them filled with water. The train crew, CB assured me, would check each time we stopped to see if I needed water. That was only partly true I would soon learn.

In each car the men had built a hayloft on one end. A supply of baled hay was stacked in each for feeding the cows. It would also be my bed for the next four nights. Sawdust was spread about six inches thick on the floor on the rail cars. We were ready to load the cows.

They came in semis that backed up to the rail cars and the heifers were driven in loose. In one boxcar a partition had been built to keep five cows separate. They were due to give birth in a few weeks and we didn't want them bumped or injured. They had access to one of the water barrels. Over all, space was pretty scarce. The boxcars were hauling all the animals they could safely hold.

Having never ridden a train, period, I had no clue as to what I was headed for. First lesson: boxcars do not ride like passenger cars, the springs are much heavier. I would also learn that under certain stressful conditions cows gave birth before their "due date." As the men were finishing putting the last planks across the doors, CB took me to a restaurant for my last meal before embarking on my five-day journey. Though I was skinny, six feet tall and only 125 pounds, I could eat a good amount. CB asked the waitress to fix me a couple of extra sandwiches and two bottles of pop to take with me. In his usual no-nonsense way he told me I'd have time to get something to eat each day as the train made frequent stops. He than gave me money to buy food for myself, a small flashlight and a return ticket to ride a passenger train back.

In the spring of 1957, you could buy a lot of food for $10.00. The problem, I would learn the very next morning, was finding food to buy.

CB's last words of advice came that day as I peered

though the planks when the switch engine hooked on. "If you have any trouble getting the yard crew to get you water, just threaten to call the yard boss."

Though it was cold outside, snowflakes still drifting intermittently to the ground, the inside of the boxcar I was in quickly warmed from the body heat given off by the cows. I was in the one where the five due cows were housed.

The big metal side doors on the car were closed! Not a lot of light crept in. I had my flashlight, but was worried I'd need it and didn't want to wear the batteries out. After being jolted back and forth, we were finally hooked to a freight train.

This was about the last days cattle were moved by train. The rules were that cattle cars were put at the front of the long line of boxcars, coal cars, tankers, etc. that made up the entire train. We were right behind the engine and power cars needed for the trip.

This was a trip of discovery from start to finish. For a naïve farm boy, the surprises came fast and often. CB had left an awful lot of space between the lines when he'd given me his brief advice and instruction.

It was late afternoon when we headed out. The water barrels were full, a wood block floating in each to cut down on the splashing from the moving boxcars. Hay mangers built from wire fence ran down each side. I could walk, very precariously, down the manger as I spread out hay for the cattle. They had been filled before we left Lansing. All I had to do was relax and enjoy the ride. I'd check the water and feed hay in the morning.

Our first major stop was Chicago. I anchored a couple of the bales to form a chair and leaned back. I was more excited than scared, wondering at the sights I'd see before this journey ended.

As the train picked up speed, I made my first unpleasant discovery. The ride was rough as hell. I was sure after about a half-hour, that I was destined to have double vision and shake up and down the for the rest of my life. The few times I'd been close to rails they looked so smooth. It would be like riding on air I thought. Looks are deceiving I reflected.

Where the sections of rail meet usually meant a bump of varying degrees. One end of the rail would sink where it met the next iron-on-iron spelling JOLT!

I spread out a little hay to make a bed. Lying down solved the problem of double vision and constant shaking. Now, however, my entire body would bounce up and down, so hard sometimes that I'd leave the bale and be briefly airborne. That was only one discovery, however.

Cold air outside, warm air from the cows inside equals condensation on the ceiling of the boxcar. Now I was bouncing up while the drops of water bounced down. At least, I told myself, it was warm rain.

Sleep was out of the question, I realized, as we sped though the dark night. It proved to be one of the longer nights of my entire life, in fact.

We stopped briefly a couple of times in the night or slowed onto a side rail to let another train pass headed the opposite way. I didn't open the doors to check where we were until the next morning when I could hear voices outside the boxcar. I rolled the big heavy metal door open about a foot and looked out. I stood there stunned! There were tracks as far as I could see in all three directions. I was in Chicago, all right, and the rail yard was massive.

It was a clear morning and not as cold as when I'd left Lansing. I checked the water barrels. The cows had not really drunk a lot, but I was feeling the responsibility for their welfare pretty strongly.

I pushed the door open wider and crawled out over top of the planks and ran to check the other car and its live content. A couple of men came walking along checking the wheels on my two cars. I told them I needed water for the cows. They just nodded and walked on by. I crawled in and checked on the cows. They were fine and had drank about the same amount of water. I got back down on the ground and waited. My two cars were setting alone. I didn't know where the rest of the train even was. There were switch engines moving freight cars constantly.

I was getting worried when another man came walking along. I was more forceful in my water request this time. I even mentioned calling the yard boss as CB had instructed me. The man just grunted and pointed to a small speaker sitting on a steel post amongst the tracks.

I walked over and looked. I pushed the button in front of me, after a few seconds a voice came through the small speaker. It was the yard boss. I explained that I needed water for the two-boxcar loads of cows I was with. He was nice and told me he'd send a switch engine to move me to where I could get water. I could see in the distance a glass-fronted tower that I figured he was watching from.

I thanked him and hurried over to my two cars. I fed hay and ate a sandwich while I waited. I now had one bottle of pop and one more sandwich left. One thing I knew, even if I were starving I was not going to leave those cows and search for food here. I was sure it must be miles to the nearest restaurant since all I could see were tracks and freight cars. In fact, there was no way I was going to let my two boxcars out of my sight even for a minute.

A switch engine came and locked on. I watched out the open door as we moved back and forth and ever sideways as switches were thrown. He parked my two cars beside a small shed. I crawled out and looked inside. I could see these huge faucets and some curled up hose about two inches in diameter. I had a bucket with me but it would take forever to fill it, climb over the planks, and dump it into the barrels. I'd have to use the hose. I hooked it up and dragged the heavy hose out and stuck the one end through the planks and into a barrel. I turned the water on and stepped outside just in time to see the hose rear up out of the barrel, spraying water everywhere. The pressure was far too high. I quickly shut it down, put the hose back in the barrel and tied it to a plank with baler twine. A lot more cautiously, I turned the handle. Even with lower force, the barrel filled quickly.

I had finished filling my last barrel and was untying the hose when I felt the jolt of the switch engine hooking on. We started moving! I quickly pushed the hose out through the planks and we were underway. It was the start of my first full day of traveling with two boxcars of cattle. I hadn't slept much, but I was excited about what lay ahead. I'd crawl down and open the door occasionally and peek outside. So far, so good.

I noticed the cows were getting tired. A few started lying down though they were in danger of getting stepped on with each sway of the train. Like me, they were getting better at keeping their legs apart for balance. The danger was in being lulled into relaxing when we'd hit a stretch of smooth track. All that would be shattered when we'd hit a particularly rough stretch. The pen that held the five cows due to calf was not as big as it should have been. One or two could lay down at a time, but I held my breath fearing they would get their udders stepped on and injured. Little did I realize that pen was going to get a lot more crowded before I got to step back on solid ground in Albuquerque, New Mexico.

The first day was pretty uneventful, for the most part. I ate my last sandwich for lunch and drank only half of my last bottle of pop. I'd need to get some food or it would be a long and hungry night.

The speed of the train continually changed as we'd slow

going through small towns. I suspect the condition of the tracks also had a great deal to do with our speed. I discovered that sitting in the hay manger, though a bit risky, was a lot smoother ride. The fence at least had a little give to it as I bounced up and down.

Viewing towns from the "back side", as you do when you ride the train, makes it hard to know where you're at. Shipping by rail was fading. Passenger travel had shrunk to a low level so towns didn't bother to put up signs. Depots sat unused and abandoned since the trains couldn't afford to stop at each to pick up passengers as they'd done in the past. CB himself stopped using trains to move cattle. When I went back to work for CB full-time five years later, we shipped all our cattle by semi trailers.

We made a few stops that day. Each time I'd climb out and look around for a place that sold food. They'd have to be a short distance from the track where I could still see my two railcars or I wasn't going. I was getting pretty hungry, but not hungry enough to risk getting left behind.

It was getting warmer, at least. I was regulating the air in each car to avoid the condensation on the roof. I needed a bath, no doubt, but water dripping on me all night was not what I had in mind.

Suppertime came and went. I'd finished the last of my pop. We'd stopped again just as it was getting dark. I jumped out and looked around for a restaurant. Nothing. I wanted to spend the night hours in the car that had the five cows separated so I could keep an eye on them. That proved a good choice since, before this night was over, I'd have something to keep my mind off food.

I'd been born on a dairy farm. In fact, literally. Mom had five of us kids in hers and Dad's bed right there in the farmhouse. I've witnessed plenty of births—from cows and pigs to sheep and kittens. I'd even had to help with several births of calves when the mothers were unable to push the calf out under their own efforts.

Farm kids don't need to be told about the birds and bees. We witnessed the whole process first hand from conception to birth.

I knew immediately what was coming when I looked in the pen and saw one cow with her tail slightly raised and swaying slightly as she lifted one hind leg and then the other. I would be adding at least one to the number of animals in my care before morning.

I picked a spot in the hay manger where I could keep an eye on the cow who was starting labor. Before long, the front legs appeared. She had still not laid down. Occasionally a first calf heifer would give birth this way. With the swaying, bouncing rail car adding to the strange atmosphere of moving, I was prepared for anything.

The head appeared, but the sack had not broken, so I knew the calf was still breathing through the mother. No need to panic yet, I wanted to tell this about to be mother that CB had said they weren't due to give birth until after we'd arrived at our destination. I figured it was a little too late for that reminder. Then the water broke!

Though I am slow to panic, my heartbeat increased considerably. The calf had to come out within the next few minutes or it would be stillborn. I climbed down into the pen.

My quick action scared the others, so a general shift in positions began. I finally managed to squeeze between them and get a hold on the two front legs. I didn't have a rope, but I knew some binder twine would work if needed for pulling.

Slippery doesn't begin to express how difficult it is to grasp and pull on an arriving calf. Though I know how much the mother appreciates the slickness in aiding the delivery, it's frustrating when you're trying to help.

Between contractions, the cow would move about. I followed, my hands never letting go of the two legs that slowly grew longer as the calf emerged. I was aware of being stepped on a couple times, squeezed against the sides occasionally, as we all did a slow wobbly dance in our cramped space.

The calf's tongue slid further out of its months from the pressure. We got past the chest, but there lies the danger. The back hips can get caught, since the mother is tiring and not pushing as hard. I grabbed the calf around its chest behind the front legs and put all my weight downward. Whoosh!

The calf, and a bunch of water, and I hit the sawdust manure mixture all at once. On my knees I worked frantically to clear the afterbirth from the calf's mouth. I pushed on its chest a few times and it started to breathe. The mother finally got turned around and mooed to the calf and began to lick it. I stood guard over the calf as the mother cleaned it from head to toe.

Baby calves are usually able to stand within ten to fifteen minutes after birth. This one tried but it could never gain its feet. I was in the pen the entire time. I was not a pretty sight. I now had sawdust, manure and fetal fluid all over me. On the positive side, I smelled just like the cows in the pen with me, which helped me blend in.

Had there been a camera in that car, I would have had several clips for America's Funniest Video.

Calves need to nurse. Since Holstein calves usually weigh around a 100 pounds at birth, it was not easy holding it up to reach the teats on a cow who moved every little bit with the lurching of the boxcar.

It took about an hour. I could now add lots of sweat to the other stuff I was covered with. I washed up in the water barrel being as careful as I could not to contaminate the water the cows had to drink.

I crawled up into the hayloft to assess the situation. I had lifted the calf over the planks and put him on the side with the younger heifers because it was a lot less crowded. His mom stood there, mooing occasionally. But she seemed to understand it was a lot safer there. She could still put her nose through and lick him

•

The gravity of the situation sunk in. I would not only have to lift that calf over to nurse every few hours, I'd have to hold him up so he could. Worse, I'd have to try and milk that cow twice a day until we arrived at our destination.

Dairy cows are bred for high milk production. They produce much more milk than their calf could consume. Hand milking a cow while bouncing and swaying down these tracks didn't sound like a whole lot of fun. However, little did I know things were going to get even worse before they got better.

I debated what to do about my clothes. I was a mess, to put it mildly. I had a clean shirt and jeans but one session of feeding the calf and trying to milk that cow would have my clean clothes looking just like the ones I had on. I decided to save them to change into when I arrived in Albuquerque.

I settled back to relax until it was time to lift the calf over to nurse. I wouldn't need to milk the cow until morning since the calf would drink most of what she had in those first several hours.

Now that the excitement was over, I realized I was hungry and thirsty. I looked down at myself and realized that even if I could find a restaurant, they'd never let me in looking and smelling like this.

Did I sleep at all on the whole trip? Well sort of. When exhaustion takes over, the body does shut down. I slept some that night. It seemed like the tracks were getting smoother as we moved steadily west and south. Just like highways, the milder weather means less maintenance, less damage during the freezing and thawing of cold weather.

As exhausted as I was, hungry and thirsty, the night- time hours seemed like the twilight zone. I'd wake and could dimly see the cows below, I'd check to make sure the calf was all right. I had him tied with binder twine, but it was unnecessary; he never tried to get up again.

I wasn't sure, as I bounced and swayed along, if I were dreaming all this or was it real. Morning and reality hit with a jolt! I realized I had slept sound after I'd fed the calf and I jumped down to check things. The calf was fine, his mom watching from the other side of the planks. I bent down to untie the twine so I could lift him over. I peered through the planks. Between the twenty legs that held the five moving and shifting cows, was another black and white shape. It was another calf! I crawled over to look. It was alive and almost dry.

Now I had two additions! I held her up to nurse. That meant convincing the mother to stand still because she'd panic when the other cows shifted and she couldn't see her baby. The calf would nurse a few seconds, then we'd envitably move again, either because the mom couldn't see and wanted to turn around, or one of the others would decide to move. I'd drag the calf along, trying to calm them all. It was not a lot of fun!

Once I felt she'd nursed enough, I'd lift her over and pick up the first calf and lift him in to his mom. Then the whole drag, shift, hold sequence started over.

I was worn out by the time I was satisfied both calves had nursed enough. They lay content on the other side of the planks. My stomach was reminding me I hadn't eaten since noon of the previous day. That situation would have to wait right now. I was faced with a new challenge. I needed to milk the cow that had had the first calf. Serious consequences could result if I didn't —milk fever being one of them.

I got my pail and crawled back into their pen. I sat my bucket in the sawdust beneath the cow. Like all mammals, the mammary glands on cows are sore at birth. They will tolerate the calf sucking on them the result of a mother's love. However, no such feeling exits between the cow and the farmer who has to milk her.

I gently rubbed her udder to get her to release her milk. Then I tried a few squeezes. Though she couldn't see me, she knew it wasn't her calf getting milk from those teats. The back leg came up to brush my hands away. Luckily, she couldn't kick hard for fear of losing her balance in the swaying bouncing motion of the train. When I hunched down to milk, the cow's bodies would close over me. All I could see were legs, manure and sawdust. I couldn't sit or kneel for fear of being stepped on.

I already had some bruises from feeding the calf. Only in memory can I see the humor in that situation. I'd get a half-inch or so of milk in the bucket only to have it kicked over by the mother or by the shifting of the cows every little while. I could now add milk to the smells collecting on my clothes. The milk smell wasn't too bad until it soured as the day progressed. I finally managed to get most of the milk, though it all ended up in the sawdust or on my pant legs as my bucket got kicked over numerous times.

•

One thing I remember very clearly, even after all these years: the further south and west I traveled the friendlier the train people became. Now, whenever we stopped at a good sized town, the crew came and checked to see if I needed water for the cows. I would be handed the hose and only had to hold it steady while the barrels filled.

I remember inquiring about a restaurant that morning after chores. I was told by the crew that there were a couple nearby. When I crawled out to look around I realized they were out of sight of my two rail cars. At 16 and in a place where I knew no one, it seemed too risky to take a chance and go find one. As hungry as I was, I was not going to let those cars out of my sight. If it went on without me, those two calves would die, not being able to nurse. I crawled back inside.

As I mentioned earlier in the story, it was hard to tell what state I was in as I rode the rails westward. I could leave the big side doors open part way now to enjoy the fresh air and scenery. The cows and I were finally getting our "train legs". They were lying down more and seemed to have accepted their fate. We all bounced and swayed down the track mile after mile without complaint.

I was getting past hungry so that didn't bother me as much. I'd caught a few sips of water from the hose as I filled the barrels that morning. I couldn't drink the cow's milk yet. I knew one sip of the rich, first milk would give me the runs for sure—not a pleasant thought under the circumstances.

When I wasn't holding the calves to nurse or feeding hay, I'd sit in the hay manger in the open door and watch the ever-changing scene flying by outside. I noticed the grass and bushes along both sides of the tracks were havens for wild life. It's where I spotted my first jackrabbit. I was astonished by their size; much larger that their cousins in Michigan. Most of the small mammals and birds would dart out and run a short ways as the train came along then they'd stop and watch.

I don't believe it rained the entire time I was traveling, the days were warm and sunny and I opened the doors farther each day. I'd switch cars frequently at first, but now, with baby calves to watch out for, I'd run to the second car, feed and check things, then hurry back before the train started up.

We'd stop occasionally, out in the middle of nowhere. I soon learned what those stops were for. We'd sit quietly for several minutes. Sometimes the engineer would walk along and say hi. We were stopped on a long siding. It was probably cheaper to build them out in the open countryside. Then I'd hear the whistle of an approaching train. It was rumbling down the main track as we waited. The first such encounter scared the cows and me too.

The two trains barely missed each other, so closely did they pass, and the noise was deafening. Then it would get quiet; I'd hear our own engines rev up and then we were moving again.

Even scarier, because I had no warning, were the times we had the right of way and another train sat quietly in a siding. I'd be watching the scenery when "bamm". I was viewing another freight train only inches from my face. I had heard and read stories about hobos who hitched rides on empty boxcars. I did see a few do just that, though I never talked to them. When we stopped at night, I'd usually see one or two men who, by appearance, were obviously not railroad workers. They never bothered me and I felt relatively safe since I didn't feel they'd care to enter a cattle car with its unique smell and atmosphere. No, that pleasure was all mine.

I still hadn't eaten as darkness fell once again. I have a habit of saying I'm all right when I'm not—a habit still with me today. I don't want to trouble other people with what I perceive as my problems. I got that from my parents and the times I grew up in. People were very independent in those rural communities I was privileged to spend my youth in. I answered the question about needing anything with my usual, "No. I'm ok." I could not risk leaving those boxcars and take a chance they'd leave without me aboard.

Shortly after dark we stopped. We were at a small rail station though I had no clue where we were. The engineer came along and said we'd be there about twenty minutes. I crawled out and walked down the board platform and went inside the station. I noticed a big jug of water. It sat in one of those containers where you took a small funnel-shaped paper cup, pushed a button, and got a drink. The cups were tiny, only a couple of swallows. I asked if I could have a drink since I didn't know if it was for the public or not. Help myself, was the answer, so I did. I didn't realize how thirsty I was until that first swallow slid down. I had mentally geared myself to deny I was hungry or thirsty. I stood there, refilling that tiny cup again and again. I didn't realize I had attracted everyone's attention until I finally stopped to catch my breath. They were all staring at me.

I blurted out that I'd run out of food and drink a day and a half ago. After a few more seconds of staring, they started looking for something to give me to eat. A few cookies were all they could find. One of the men went and got a full bottle of water and helped me get it over the planks and up in the hayloft. I now had enough water for the rest of the trip. One of the men asked what I'd like to eat. He'd order it for me and it would be waiting at our next stop. That's how it went for the rest of my trip. I'd order things and they'd be ready when we stopped again. I never had to worry about something to eat for the rest of the trip. Looking back I realize the word probably spread that some kid was riding with these two boxcars full of cows without any food or water. The train people watched out for me from then on,

The next twenty-four hours were highlighted by two more animals in what had become the "birthing wing" of the boxcar. On the plus side, both were alive and healthy. On the down side, I now had four cows to milk and there were four afterbirths sacks tangled into the manure and sawdust, and the temperature was getting hotter. Even if I had brought along a bottle of after-shave, it wouldn't have made a dent into the growing aroma inside those boxcars

At the time, I barely noticed. I was a farm boy...a farm boy who had cleaned hog barns, chicken coops, horse stables, and shoveled the gutters in the cow barn daily. This was all perfectly normal. I had hoped to find the afterbirth sacks and throw them out, but never did.

Helping the four calves nurse and milking the cows took a great deal of my time now. Still, I got to sit in the manger and stare out at the countryside as we bounced and swayed along. We were in the desert now. There were huge rivers running under the tracks, but completely void of water. I learned later that they were only huge runoffs when it rained. We'd slow down though the small towns, which seemed to get further and further apart. We were slowly going through one such town when this group of boys spotted me sitting in the open door way. I became an instant target to see who could hit me with a rock. Several bounced off the side of the car as the boys ran along side the train. It was a small, brief lesson in human nature. I remained in my lofty perched as they slowly faded from view.

It was my only negative encounter of the entire trip. I was enjoying myself, enjoying the new sights that every mile seemed to bring. Since sleep wasn't easy on those cars, I did very little of it. I had all four doors locked open and sat in the manger day and night between chores. Those open doors not only lifted my spirit, but did a lot with refreshing the air inside.

I settled into a routine of sorts. Now that I didn't' have to worry about something to eat or getting adequate water for the cows, my main focus was on getting those calves and cows to Albuquerque in a good as shape as possible.

I had not communicated with anyone other than the railroad employees I'd encountered along the way. No word to my parents, no checking on me by CB or his secretary. That all seemed perfectly normal to everyone in 1957. I felt in no danger; it was an adventure and, despite the arrival of the calves and the extra work, I was loving every minute. I felt perfectly at home with farm animals of all kinds. It never occurred to me that I could easily have been trampled down below the cows trying to milk. One misstep could have led to serious injury or worse. I could have fallen from my hay manger and laid alongside the tracks for days before anyone found me. I don't recall any of those kind of thoughts, though I'm sure I was always watchful and careful. Something I'd been taught since birth.

The lush fields and woods of the Midwest states had given way to miles of cactus and sandy, bare soil. The jackrabbits became more plentiful by the hour. They would hop out from the vegetation beside the track and sit and watch as we rolled by. It was in stark contrast to the area I had grown up in. I'd see range cattle occasionally, but couldn't figure out how they found enough to eat out there to even survive. On our farm in Michigan grass grew everywhere. Even the narrow strips between the road and our fence line could feed several cattle all summer. It was obvious why the western farms or ranches were so big. It took several acres just to support one cow.

I knew this part of my journey was coming to an end. The trainmen had told me we'd arrive at our destination in the late evening. As we rolled to a stop I could see cattle pens. There were dozens of them as far as I could see. A switch engine took me in front of one and left me. It was as big as our entire barnyard at home. Fresh water glistened in the large tanks. A yardman came with a crow bar and helped me get the planks off one side on each car, gates guided the cows down ramps and onto solid ground at last. It was funny watching the cows reaction; they walked slowly, stopping to sniff and look around. Then, with wobbly, teetery legs still not used to solid footing, they finally got down to the dirt part. More sniffing and looking around. A few walked slowly to the water troughs. Finally one or two, realizing they were indeed on real dirt again, began to run and jump. Slowly, that feeling spread through them all. There were cows running, jumping and kicking in all directions.

I watched and laughed, caught up in their joy at being on a familiar feeling turf again. I waited until they settled down before I carried the calves down the ramp and put them on the ground beside their mothers. They all seemed healthy, but I sure wanted to see them get up and walk and hopefully nurse on their own.

One by one they did. I had gotten my things off the rail car and was sitting on the board fence when these men came walking over. They were the men who had purchased the cows from CB back in Michigan. This was their first "live" inspection of the cattle CB had chosen for them. They seemed pleased as I followed them around the pen. They had lots of questions about how I had managed to keep four calves alive and in good condition under those circumstances. We shared some laughs at my efforts at hand milking while the train had bounced and swayed along.

I was invited to stay at the farm with them for as long as I wanted. They offered to buy me something to eat. I was by now needing only one thing—a shower—the sooner the better. A shower and a night's sleep on a bed that didn't bounce and sway.

Next morning I went out and watched them milk their large herd of dairy cows. There were no barns like I was used to. A shed housed the milking area and equipment. Since they had no winter, the cows stayed out year around. After breakfast I asked if someone could drive me into Albuquerque so I could look around. They had already called CB and told him of the excellent condition the cows had arrived in including the four newborns. They even offered me a job to stay and work for them. I wasn't even tempted at the good pay or the absence of cold weather. Somewhere in my future was a newspaper. I wanted to own one so I could print what I wanted. I wasn't sure when or where that would happen, but I knew it would.

I can't remember a whole lot about Albuquerque. I felt out of place, I know. Partly, I suppose because I didn't know a single soul in the entire city. Quite a switch from the secluded farm community I'd grown up in where we all knew each other. I got some unfriendly stares and watchful suspicious looks a I wondered the streets. There was not a single thing that would be familiar to me now. Like other American cities, the Albuquerque I saw in 1957 has been swallowed up by growth and progress. I do remember how different it felt there. The pace was slower. I'd never seen that many people lounging and standing around during the day.

I pride myself on being an above-average observer. Where and how we grow up shapes us for life. So do our experiences as we grow into adults. This trip, though I didn't consciously think about it at the time, was the start of an attitude I would carry for life. No matter whether it was something for myself or someone else, I would ask certain things of myself. When I went beyond what was expected, I was doing if for myself, not my employer or my parents. If I wanted real self-esteem, I had to earn it the hard way – by satisfying myself, by meeting the standards I set for myself. It has made even the thousand mundane tasks I've done rewarding.

It was time to head home. I had first class passenger tickets this time. To my disappointment, those cars with their recliner seats weren't a whole lot smoother ride than my hayloft in the box cat. I still had trouble sleeping. We did go a lot faster with less stopping, so the trip home seemed a lot shorter. I realize now that it was the ending of passenger train service. The tracks were in disrepair. Only a few other people shared the car I rode in. An industry was slowly dying.

I don't remember who picked me up in Lansing or how I got back to our farm. I only know there was no big to-do on my arrival. I was back in my farm clothes doing chores within an hour of my arrival. The stories were shared later, a little at a time. I had merely done as expected. I had cared for the animals to the best of my ability. That was simply my responsibility, after all.

Harry, Carl, Lassie and Geo. Jr.

C.B. Smith, auctioneer. Herb Miller on his right.

Working for
the auctioneer,
C.B. Smith

CB, as everyone respectfully called him, was a unique man. He had been born in Kentucky, but had built his life in Williamston, Michigan, a small town not far from the capitol of Lansing. He was a licensed auctioneer, dabbled in real estate, but his passion was Holstein dairy cattle. I had know him for years before I went to work for him full time in the summer of 1959. My family had purchased many of our herd of registered Holsteins from CB, himself, through his auctions.

He had built a beautiful sale barn near Williamston. It had offices, apartments above, a restaurant below, a large sales arena, wash bay, bunk rooms, showers, a big area for housing the sale animals and a comfort stall barn and milk house for his own animals all under one roof. There was a huge haymow above the area that held the cattle. It was his little empire and he had great pride in it.

He had monthly dairy cattle auctions there. He also did farm auctions. Most of his auctions involved a herd of registered Holsteins. CB had earned a several-state reputation for getting good prices and knowing how to market good dairy cows.

Dairymen consigned animals to his sales and CB also covered Michigan, Indiana and Ohio as well as Canada in search of good cows or bulls, which he would purchase and then turn around and sell at the monthly auction. He had a great eye for judging, especially finding "diamonds in the rough." He would spot a cow or heifer with potential that might not look good right then or be at their prime. He took great delight in purchasing animals for a low price and later leading them to first place at the local and state shows. Then he would put them in special sales where they would bring many times the price he paid. He always had a glint in his eye when relating to me how little he had paid for an animal and what they sold for later.

He was also, by nature, an intimidating man. People were generally afraid of him and maybe a little in awe of his personality and his seemingly natural ability and energy. He was a man you would always remember even if you crossed his path only briefly. I never knew a lot about his past, only that he'd been a factory worker at one time. The world he had created—the man he was when our paths crossed—was a good place for me to be at that time. I was twenty when I hired on full time at $300.00 per month—that was seven days a week, and ten to twelve hours a day. We had two days off per month and only did chores on Sundays. That was good pay for then, even though the hours were long.

I was quite an individual myself at age twenty, but in a quiet way. I was not intimidated by, nor afraid of CB. I think that was why a trust and mutual respect developed during my time there. Dad and I had talked about working for CB when I was considering it. We knew there was a high turnover of workers at the sales pavilion. We'd see new faces each time we went to a sale. Even the managers CB hired didn't stay long. That didn't bode well when looking for a long term, secure job. Still, Dad had great respect for CB and felt he would be fair and a man of his word. My two younger brothers could handle helping Dad on the farm, so off I went.

I guess introspective would be a good word to describe me during that period of my life. I wasn't sharing my thoughts with anyone but I was thinking some pretty heavy ones trying to figure the world out. Being completely on my own was good. I didn't have a girlfriend, wasn't even dating anyone. My life to that point had revolved around the family farm. I had read Ayn Rand's Fountainhead and had figured out enough about people to see the serious errors in some of her assumptions of people. There are shades of gray in us all, even if we try to live life in strictly black and white. Still, she was the first writer to take me down mental roads I had not traveled before. I wished I were in New York and could attend her sessions with young intellectuals, not to sit and raptly listen, but to challenge some of her conclusions about human nature and what motivates us.

I wonder what direction my life would have taken if I'd done that. Some people marvel at all I've done in my life—chances I've taken and such. I think about all the chances I didn't take, opportunities I let slip by. I am not a person who thinks back and regrets – that would be second-guessing myself. But somewhere inside me is a voice reminding me I only go around once and I should have taken more of those chances.

There was a boarding house in Williamston where I got a room; it was right on main street. I don't recall what it cost but it was cheap. There were two other "roomers" living there. Even before hiring in at CB's, I had wanted to get my own car. I had been driving a 1947 maroon Dodge four door. Not a cool car even for teenager's back then, I had my eye on a 1959 Plymouth Fury. I wanted a brand new one with a stick shift. My friend Gary Willoughby had a 1958 Chevy stick shift and had done well in the little bit of drag racing we did. My Dodge with fluid drive was not exactly a racing legend. It was a great family sedan however. Thinking back, my dad, George was unique in lots of ways, especially for those times. I had already moved to Williamston and liked my job. Dad offered to find my 1959 Fury and I could make the payments. The 1960 models had come out, which I didn't like near as well. Dad couldn't find my stick shift fury with the big engine. He called one day and said he'd found a Chevy Impala convertible, stick shift. It was blue with a white top and had the big engine. The idea grew on me so dad drove it up to me. It cost $2800 and it was one of my all time favorite cars.

I remember feeling like a misfit when I started at C.B.'s I didn't even look like a farm boy. I wore shirts that I had cut the sleeves off and tennis shoes. I knew no one except C.B. and he and I had rarely spoken. I only had his initial respect from the job I had done riding the freight cars full of cows to New Mexico a few years before.

I barley weighed 120 lbs. thought I was six feet tall. One of the other employees, a rough talking man named Mike, teased me. Told me I had traded legs with a stork and got beat out of my ass. Then he'd laugh so hard spittle would form in the corners of his mouth. I liked him though and he soon looked up to me and my ability. The manager at the time was Charlie Baker.

He and his wife lived in one of the apartments above the offices. He had retired and sold his big dairy herd and CB had talked him into getting this place shaped up. He was slow and meticulous. Two traits CB had little patience with. I think he lasted about six mouths. I did learn some new things from him about milking cows with udder problems. He did know his stuff. Another employee reminded me of the big strong, not too bright character in "Of Mice and Men". His name was Irvin. He was a good worker and would grin at me whenever I complimented him. We also had part time workers. CB would pick some up and bring them to work at the sales. Don't know where he found them, but most would last one day – they didn't care to work that hard, especially dealing with all those cattle at the monthly sale.

Almost every month, CB would import one or two semi loads of cows from Canada. He would drive from farm to farm up there and purchase the animals he liked. They would arrive at the sale barn, loose in their trailer and packed tight. Our job was to put a rope halter on each, lead them down an outdoor ramp and tie them in a designated area in the sale barn. That was easier said than done! Most had never had a halter on nor been tied by one. They were used to walking into a barn with stanchions which would close loosely on their neck so they could freely eat and drink. It was about 20 to 30 feet from the end of the ramp to the barn door. The trick was to sort of guide them until you got inside the barn and then pull the halter tight and try to get them tied. That was when all hell broke loose.

The first time I had to help with this job one man would open the truck door, then try to get a halter on them one by one. That only worked while they were tightly packed. As soon as we got a few out, the rest had room to move and it was almost impossible to get a halter on one. I have always been innovative, so I suggested we halter them all before we started. Since it was my idea and I was the lightest, I got to crawl in on their backs and do the job. It worked remarkably well. They couldn't move much, and they liked to keep their heads up so they could see. One of the other men would throw me halters as I sat on their backs. I would slip one on and loop the long end over their neck. In just a few minutes the 12 to 15 cows all had halters on. I'd crawl out over theirs backs.

Sometimes we would double up—two of us holding on to the rope—as we led the cow down the ramp. A danger point was getting into the barn door ahead of the cow. The ropes weren't long enough if you were behind, and you'd likely get squeezed good if you were beside them when they went through the door. Some would hit the ground running, some you had to push in.

This job is where we lost most of our part-time helpers; usually they had never worked with cows and the sight of those 1200 pound cows charging down the ramp dragging the helpless man who was supposed to be leading them didn't seem worth the pay, I'm sure.

I preferred to lead one alone; whatever she did, I didn't have to worry about falling over someone else who didn't move the right way or fast enough. My 120 pounds was no match for them on dirt but, once they hit the cement, I could turn them. Their hooves slid on the cement, though they still had lots of power in their weight. I got really good at pulling at the right time and using their weight to my advantage.

The next exciting thing was having to milk them. No farmer is going to tell CB, when he's looking at cows and making an offer, that they were kickers or they are used to one kind of milker, etc. We were on our own. Many times, the milking machine and I both landed out in the walkway. I learned to stand, legs apart, head pushed into their flank as I put the milker on. I could feel the first bit of movement with my head and I could push, keeping them off balance so they couldn't kick me too hard. It takes both hands to put the suction cups on each teat.

We usually had between 150 and 200 head of cattle in each sale. They all had to have a bath, head to toe. There was a wash rack next to the area the cows were tied in. We'd lead them in, tie them to a pipe and start. Summertime wasn't too bad— they had shed their winter coat and the heavy shit that was usually stuck to it. The rack held four or five head at a time. Two men would usually wash and a couple more would lead them in and out and give them clean bedding for their return. After one was washed, we'd place a flannel sheet over them so the hair would look nice once it dried.

Of course this washing business was also new to most of the cows. They didn't like it any better than they did being tied.

I was always careful to not get water in their ears. Other men didn't share my concern and sprayed water wildly rather than stand beside them and cover one ear then the other as they washed and rinsed their head. Since we wanted the cows to look their best on sale day, I thought it was a traumatic enough experience the cows were enduring without the discomfort of water in their ears.

In order to get the cows clean, you had to use a scrub brush on every inch, especially their legs, feet and belly which were the dirtiest. You used a bucket of soapy water for that and then rinsed them with a hose. I usually washed because I could do it faster.

We only had two or three days to get all those cattle clipped and washed for sale day. (I'll describe the clipping part next.)

I'd put on rubber boots and my worst pants and shirt for wash day. Invariably, a good bit of shit that came off the cows got on the man washing them. The tails were the worst. They would be matted with shit and once they got wet they became foul smelling lethal weapons. The more nervous the washing made them, the more they switched their tails in response. As anyone who has worked with animals will tell you, when they get nervous their bowels kick in. The soupy shit would hit the wet cement and fly everywhere. I'm sure your mind is imagining how I looked at the end of a 12-hour day having washed 50 to 70 cows. Only pictures would do it justice. It's probably just as well I didn't have a girlfriend back then. If she'd have paid a surprise visit to see me on wash day that probably would have been the end of her urge to hug and kiss me.

As I mentioned earlier, every sale animal had to be clipped. It was an art that greatly enhanced an animal's appearance. I had clipped show animals for 4-H and local B&W shows. At CB's I learned all the tricks those clippers could do in the hands of a skilled herdsman. I became quite good at it, as did my brother Carl who came later and also worked for CB.

Some of the top showmen from around the country would accompany their sale animals to CB's. I'd watch and learn. We'd start with the tail first, especially if the cow had never been clipped. That helped them get used to the noises.

Still, as with people, animals all have personalities and traits unique to themselves. Some would practically fall asleep as I clipped and pampered them. Others would move side to side and fight me the whole time. The more I learned about judging dairy cattle from CB, the better I became with the clippers to accent their good traits and hide their bad ones. We'd leave a nice bushy tail, trim up and over the top of their rumps to make them straighter on top. If it was a milking cow, we'd trim their belly to show the huge milk veins running to the udder. The skin on the udder itself was very pliable and thin. You had to be very careful or the clippers would nick and draw blood.

You clipped the entire neck and worked back to the

shoulders to blend them in. The judge looked for sharpness on the shoulders and a lean dairy looking neck and head. You basically clipped from the shoulder blade to the tip of their nose. Most didn't care to have their ears clipped inside and out. The loud clippers didn't help.

What a difference it all made though. I guess you'd compare it today to those "extreme makeover" shows. It was fun to watch the farmers' faces when they came on sale day to see how much their animal brought. That dirty, scruffy animal they'd dropped off was now shining, clipped and hardly recognizable. It almost made them want to take it back home.

CB had his own standards, his own criteria for how the animals looked, and how the sales arena looked. Everything had to look right. It was how he'd developed the reputation as being one of the best auctioneers in the country.

As I mentioned early on, CB was hard to work for; he expected a lot. He had little patience for slackers or something done half-assed. My Dad was the some way. He'd raised us in an environment that reflected how much care and pride he had in his farm and how things were done. While CB's other employee's looked at their job as too demanding, too hard, I saw it as a challenge.

I have received many compliments over my lifetime. Recognition received for many different reasons, but the one I got from CB has remained vivid in my mind. It was unique in that it was never verbalized. Most people wouldn't even recognize it as a compliment, but the way I view things. It was one of the best I've ever gotten.

CB approached me one day and stated that he'd like to start his own dairy show herd as he'd done several times before. He wondered if I'd be interested in being the herdsman if he did. I would be in charge of them myself. Manager Charlie and most of the men who were there when I started were long gone. I quickly answered that I would. I felt I still had a lot to learn and this was an excellent place to learn it.

Being a herdsman for anyone had never been my goal, not even for my Dad. My passion for writing smoldered inside and, along with it, a desire to make the world a better place through my writing and editing for a newspaper. I'd been reading books at a fast pace since I'd moved to CB's. I was now living in one of the apartments above the office. I had only to walk out my door, down the stairs, across the sales pavilion and I was where the cows were. Didn't even have to step outside. I didn't have a TV; didn't want one. I was reading books like the "The

Rise and Fall of the Third Reich" and books on Communism; I was trying to understand how we got to where we were as people and where we might be headed, especially America. I even wrote down some thoughts and conclusions I'd reached. While my urge to be a great writer was growing, I also enjoyed the physical labor I was performing at CB's. Once a farm boy, always a farm boy, they say.

Back to my compliment from CB: He started buying cows and heifers with a passion. It seemed my show barn of comfort stalls was filling up fast. CB was a hands-on instructor. There were always quick lessons on how to do things right. I was intent on doing it exactly the way he wanted and expected since I viewed it as a learning experience. He showed me things like bedding the front feet a little higher, how to fluff their tails out, how to feed a little hay at a time so they'd eat more and waste less.

Every morning he'd arrive about 7 a.m. He lived in a fancy house in Williamston but I suspect it was because his wife made him. CB would have been fine in the bunkroom near the cows. He'd head to the barn first. He'd walk in, look around and then offer tips or point out things I hadn't done.

I was now getting up at 4 a.m. just so I could get things looking good before he got there. I had to milk first, then shovel all the shit out of the gutters, brush all the cows, wash their tails, put fresh bedding, down, feed them silage, grain and hay… it was a long list done daily.

He didn't want visitors walking in without his private herd looking their best. Day after day it was the same—no matter how good I thought everything looked, he'd find something to comment on. Most people, I guess, would have given up on ever pleasing him. He never said something looked good; only pointed out where it needed improvement.

On sale days I'd get down to the barn sometimes at 2 a.m. We would have lots of buyers and just lookers that day and his herd had to be the highlight – he'd bring people through the barn, pointing out his recent purchases and their hidden potential. He had a voice that carried all over the barn. He didn't need a microphone.

The show barn was separated from all the sale barn area by a cement block wall. I was in my own little world until the door slid open and someone came in. On that particular day I'd gotten my usual start. The barn was clean, the walkways all swept, fresh bedding in the stalls, fresh shavings on the walk behind the cows. Their tails were washed and fluffed, the cows brushed. It looked good.

I was feeding hay by hand, a little at a time, when CB walked in. He always wore a scowl and always walked fast. I'd compare him to watching a locomotive charging down the tracks. He was a good-sized man and just watching him was impressive enough without him having to say a word. His eyes took in every detail. He looked at the cows, the walks, at me feeding hay. I stopped feeding to listen to whatever he might point out that wasn't quite right this time. Our eyes met for just a second, then he turned and left the barn, shutting the door behind him. Not a word had been uttered by either of us. CB was not in the habit of saying good morning and neither was I.

I stood there stunned for a moment. Then a feeling of elation swept over me, I had done it! I had everything so right he couldn't find anything to criticize. I was on that high most of the day. I needed no verbal compliment. I had pleased myself.

I look around at our society now and I see people who can't even breathe on their own without constant positive reinforcement. They wouldn't have lasted a day at CB's with the overuse of compliments today.

Kids need to hear they've done well as well as what they did wrong. I compliment my children a lot. But what I want––what's important—is that they do it to please themselves. Self-created self-esteem will be the rock that supports them through life. Artificial praise for mediocre effort will not build inner strength. That's a hollow victory.

•

I traveled quite a bit in the short time I worked for CB. I'll try to recall some of those trips. We made three or four trips to southern states and a few to western states—these were all by truck. CB no longer used trains. I also got to attend some cow shows with his growing private herd. Whenever CB shipped cattle to other states, I usually accompanied them. It would be called the Alabama State sale or Louisiana State sale, etc., but CB provided most of the cattle. They were usually bred heifers or young cows ready to calf. It was usually two semi-trailers full, about twenty-five head. CB had his own truck too—a Chevy two-ton stake truck. It had overdrive and I put lots of miles on it.

One trip was all bred heifers. There was a man in Michigan who bought and raised calves and then sold them again when they were ready to freshen with their first calf. The problem was he never spent any time around them; they were loose on pasture until the semis arrived to bring them to CB's. To say they were wild was an understatement. They were rounded up, funneled through an outdoor loading chute, and each given a shot of tranquilizer as they entered the semi. They arrived at CB's drugged and barely mobile.

We'd get them in the barn and tie them with two halters per CB's instructions. Once the tranquilizers wore off it was pandemonium. They would throw themselves, jerk, jump, some even bloodied their heads against the partition planks they were tired to. I'd stand watch in case one rolled and started choking. A few I had to cut loose with a jackknife and put on new halters. For some, I'd have to cut the halter off later since it wouldn't loosen because of the dried blood.

I usually had only a week, at most, to get them used to people, trained to lead, and then it was back on the truck for a thirty- or forty-hour trip south. There they were clipped, washed and CB expected them to lead well in the sale ring.

Not a job for animal rights activists, huh? Some were so wild I couldn't even walk up and touch them. They'd kick or thrash and try to get away. I'd spend almost all my time with them until it was time to head south. I had to feed them in rubber tubs, lead each one to water at least twice a day, and began getting them used to being touched and handled.

That was a full time job to say the least. Surprisingly, some responded to my kindness, the feed, etc, right away. Others I had to watch, especially around their back legs.

When the semis arrived it was ready-or-not. I'd gotten to know each one's personality by then. How best to handle them and their quirks, I was the only human they were used to at that point. They had begun to trust me.

CB always wanted me to care for the animals that were his. He'd even tell some of the other workers to stay away from them. With this particular bunch of heifers, that didn't hurt anyone's feelings. The rest didn't want to get anywhere near the wild bunch.

We had two semi loads. I packed a few clothes and climbed in the cab of one and we were on the road. We had one company we always hired to truck our cattle. They were experienced with hauling livestock and were careful of their cargo. Besides, as I've stated, people were afraid of CB and they sure didn't want to tell him one of his cows got hurt in transit.

This would have been the summer of 1961. I liked riding in the cab of the big semis, especially as we got further south. We traveled a lot of two-lane highways. Expressways were few and far between. One driver was quiet, rarely spoke; he smoked a cigar the whole time, or rather smoked half and chewed the other half until they met in the middle. The other was jolly and talkative. I got in the cab with him, as he offered and the quiet one didn't.

I-94 from Detroit to Chicago had just opened and we headed down US-27 until we picked it up. I remarked that I'd always wanted to drive a semi. I had a special license so I could legally drive CB's two-ton straight truck. Next thing I knew, the driver pulled over and said, "Here." I got behind the wheel and started down the highway. It drove like a Cadillac. I was elated! So many gears! It was air-assist shifting, so each time I moved the big lever a "hiss" would sound.

He suggested we stop at a rest area up ahead. The two trucks always stayed right together the whole trip. I slowed down and put my foot on the big brake pedal. It was like an oversized gas pedal. I kept pushing a little further, nothing happened, we were coming up on the exit pretty fast. I pushed and pushed. The driver was getting a little nervous and so was I. I pushed harder and all at once it caught and we jerked. He told me to let up. The trick was to push hard at first, then ease up and let the air do its job. Brave man that he was, he continued to let me drive.

By day's end, I was getting pretty confident. Drivers back then had all these signals they gave each other when they met on the road. They could warn each other about everything from an accident ahead to a cop with radar.

I mostly loved driving along the rolling hills, as it required lots of shifting gears. Then there were all the small towns. I'd shift in a low gear, with black smoke from the diesel and everyone looking at us as we drove through. There's a little "ham" in us all.

Halfway to our destination we stopped at a cattle farm. We unloaded and let the heifers drink and stretch. Then it was back on the road again.

The sale was held in a stadium. The heifers were put in an area below the bleachers. I clipped and washed them. CB and Miss Lynn arrived by car. Miss Lynn was CB's secretary and all-around assistant. She was a character, herself, and they worked well together. I'll have more to tell about her later.

I remember an incident while CB was putting numbers on my "wild" heifers. As I said, they trusted me now, but were still leery of strangers. He stuck a number on one heifer's hip and she promptly kicked him hard in the thigh area. "Whoa, now" was all he said as he continued more cautiously down the line.

Sale day I had them shined and looking good. I had

them started on beet pulp, which was a byproduct of sugar beets. They could eat a lot and not get sick like they would from grain. It swelled when it got wet and most cows would develop a taste for it. A full-sized cow could eat two bushels with no ill effects.

I had to lead them quite a ways to the sale ring. As the stadium was in a big circle, I couldn't see the auction ring. CB had hired a couple of young black men to help lead them to the ring while I prepped them.

That was wishful thinking. There were two problems. These men were strangers in the heifer's eyes, and they had never been around cattle so up close and personal. I showed them how to lead—stay close to the animal so they wouldn't get away.

The first started out and quickly disappeared in the circle of the walls. In no time the heifer came running back—alone. I ended up leading them all myself. They were scared and would lean against me as we walked. My feet took a real beating that day.

We drove back in CB's black station wagon. He drove like he did everything else—fast. I was in the back seat hoping for the best. I've witnessed CB passing a cop while going over the speed limit. When he'd get along side, he'd glare over at the policeman for a second. We never got pulled over.

In fact, some time later the police chief from Williamston came out to the auction barn. CB wasn't there but the police chief wanted to talk to Miss Lynn. I happened to be in the office talking to her. The chief asked Miss Lynn if she'd ask CB to slow down in the city limits. They were all afraid to stop him, so they hoped he'd listen to her. We laughed about it after the chief left.

Miss Lynn did tell CB to slow down and I think he did. He had great respect for her advice.

I remember one other stop on the trip back. We stopped for coffee, black. I was feeling quite grown up so I ordered coffee too, though I didn't then and still don't, drink it on a regular basis. The coffee came. I need milk and sugar in abundance in mine. Before I could even get mine stirred, CB had downed his in three gulps.

We were sitting at the counter. I took a sip and burned my lips and tongue. I tried stirring and blowing all the while aware that CB was ready to go. I learned never to order anything when I was with him that I couldn't gulp down quickly.

On a later trip south, my brother Carl was along. He had also hired in at CB's. We drove the stake truck this time and followed the two semi's. In our truck we were carrying the sales arena and a few heifers. One was almost pure white and had horns. Carl— or "Butch" as we all called him—and I didn't like this heifer and we were sure glad to be taking her to be sold. She was as mean and contrary as any animal as I'd ever seen.

When the sale was over and we were loading up the arena, C.B came to tell us we had one to take back. He'd tried to get more money and had gotten stuck with her. You guessed it!

We were both complaining and cussing our luck as we loaded her up to head back to Michigan. She did finally sell in one of the regular monthly sales.

•

In 1961 there was a big difference in the price of things between the north and south, you could get a breakfast for 75 cents down south. It would cost two or three dollars in Michigan.

The same with the motel rooms. The songs in the jukebox were several months behind the ones in Michigan. Those differences don't exist now.

I've already written about one trip south that made me aware of racism first hand. I won't recount that trip here.

On my first trip out west, three things happened that could have been a serious blow to my well-being mentally and physically. The same two truck drivers manned the semis as we headed to Arizona. A day and a half from our destination I began to feel bad. I had cramps and felt sick to my stomach. I was riding with the quiet one this time and tried to hide my discomfort. I remember having brief fits of sleep as we rolled through the darkness. I'd look over and my driver would be sitting ramrod straight with that cigar clamped in his teeth. I had to stop a few times with diarrhea. Both drivers were good about it.

We rolled into a deserted fairground in late afternoon. I was weak and sick. The quiet driver would not help unload cattle. He'd open and shut the tailgate as I haltered them and led them out. The jolly one pitched in and helped some because he felt bad for me. He'd lead one after I haltered it. Luckily, they weren't the crazy, wild ones.

I would realize later it wasn't stomach flu. I had a serious case of food poisoning. We finally got the cattle unloaded and tied.

The drivers, especially the jolly one, were worried as I was getting weaker by the hour. They had a schedule and I assured them I was fine. Some officials for the sale were due to arrive at the fairgrounds in the morning.

They left and I set about watering and feeding the cattle. I'd carry two pails and then have to sit and rest. I went to the bathroom and realized I was passing pure blood, instead of stool. I finally finished and collapsed on some bales of hay. I felt too bad to care right then if I lived or died. I didn't bother to even look to see if there was a working phone booth somewhere on the fairgrounds. It was isolated – no houses or building nearby.

Next morning I felt a little better, but still so weak I could only stand a few minutes at a time. I fed and watered, then rested awhile. I had to clip and wash my heifers and help set up the sale ring all in the next two days.

CB and Miss Lynn were flying down for the sale about mid morning the next day. A cattle truck arrived with more cows. A man accompanied these as I had ours. They were from California. He had only about a fourth as many cattle and he offered to help with mine. He was in his mid 40s, I guessed, and did things like this for a living.

I was slowly feeling better, though I wasn't ready to try eating yet. I clipped some of mine while he watched. I wouldn't let him help as I didn't know if his work would please CB. If he botched a cow up with a bad clipping job, CB would be upset.

Since I was still a naïve, quiet farm boy, I would have stayed at the fair grounds until someone came with food. This other man had been doing this a long time. When we finished for the day, he called a cab to pick us up to go into town to eat. The group putting on the auction still hadn't showed up. This other herdsman and I were the only ones there.

At dinner he began telling me about himself. He was married, had a couple kids. I politely listened as the story got darker and darker. He had arranged everything and on his way home was planning to kill himself. I was horrified. He started crying and hugging me. He insisted I go with him while he called his wife for a final goodbye. I believed every word and was trying my best to talk him out of it, pointing out all he had to live for etc.

When we got back to the fairgrounds I was emotionally drained. He had made up his place to sleep near mine. He started crying again and came and laid by me. I tried to comfort him until he tried to kiss me and his hands were touching my legs and thighs. I still could not believe he wasn't serious about killing himself. I'd try and stop him without hurting his feelings.

He eventually gave up and crawled back to his space. No mention was made about it again.

It sounds funny here in this day and age when even young people know about homosexuality, but back then I didn't.

When the sale was over I still believed he was going to commit suicide and I felt bad because I hadn't talked him out of it. I was still trying. The next year I saw him at a big cow show in Chicago. He had a teenaged boy with him and I finally figured it out. He had been telling the truth about his wife and kids however; I learned that from some people who knew him.

Post script: Here in 2005 as this story is being prepared for publication, I felt I needed to share my thoughts of today reflecting all I have learned about human sexuality since the events in this story took place. I believe, and have no doubt it will be scientifically proven in the next several years, that human sexuality is determined in the womb before birth. Whether we are hetrosexual, homosexual or any degree in between, is determined by our individual chemical and genetic makeup. It's not a choice nor a sin, but a naturally occuring trait of humans and many other species. I do not want to be remembered as a person who added fuel to the fire of prejudice and hysteria already rampant in our society based on a centuries old myth.

•

After the sale, CB had plane tickets for he, Miss Lynn and myself. I had never been in an airplane and was plenty nervous. It was propeller driven but quite big. We boarded in late evening and would be flying mostly at night. CB and Miss Lynn sat in the two seats on the left of the isle. I sat opposite and took the window seat—no one else sat in the aisle seat beside me. It was only four seats across.

It bothered my ears some, but I don't think they flew near as high as they do now. We had been in the air a while when it began to get bumpy. I could see lighting out my window but had no idea where we were, how high, etc. The stewardess came and told us to be sure to stay in our seats and checked to make sure we were buckled in.

It got rougher and rougher—I could tell Miss Lynn was getting scared. CB was his usual self and just winked at me that all was OK.

I don't have any idea how many feet we would drop but I'd feel like I was hanging in mid air, held only by my seat belt. I still wasn't scared; I figured flying was normally like this. After we'd drop, we felt like we'd go back up as I'd sink into my seat cushion. We dropped again and Miss Lynn screamed, just a small, short one. I looked over and noticed CB's glasses had came up out of his suit coat pocket and were hanging freely in the air. He only wore them to read. I realized at the same time there was quite a bit of air between my ass and the seat below. I had never been one to go on carnival rides because I didn't care for the feeling that was now in my stomach.

I didn't get any reassuring looks from CB that time. We were all holding on for dear life. Things finally settled down and CB retrieved his glasses from the isle floor. The stewardess came by and said we were making an unscheduled stop ahead to put the plane's contents back together. It was good to feel solid ground, though we stayed in our seats. The rest of the trip was OK.

•

Miss Lynn had been CB's secretary and all-around assistant for years before I became an employee. She was not at all intimidated by CB. In fact, she was one of only a few people with nerve enough to call CB by his real name, Clarence.

She single-handedly kept that large business and its many details straight. She was a no-nonsense individual. She had the straight-laced look of a school marm. She had never married. She took a liking to this skinny, polite, naïve farm boy and I'm forever grateful she did. She watched out for me, and she was a sympathetic ear when I needed one. Had she been there the day CB put me on that train with only two sandwiches and two bottles of pop a few years earlier, she'd have seen I had plenty of food to take along. When I finally quit to go back to finish high school, CB gave me an extra check to help. I suspect Miss Lynn was probably behind that too.

•

CB's new show herd was slowly taking shape. We entered some in the State Fair. These I trucked there in CB's own truck, making a couple of trips. Like everything else he did, CB wanted his show string to look their best.

I was getting into the groove of making animals look their best. It was a very competitive show atmosphere back then. There were many dairy herds and they were serious about winning. There would be 300 head or more at the shows. Many of those herds have disappeared like our own and been replaced by "milk factories" where individual animals mean nothing.

CB had sent me to the Graham School for reproductive problems in cows the first year I worked for him. I drove my '60 Chevy to Garrett Kansas, sat in a classroom, and then it was hands-on work with infertile cows.

CB had bought a couple of really good cows cheap because the owners couldn't get them with calf. He hoped I would learn to treat them when I got back so we'd get them bred, show them, and sell for a big profit.

I was successful with all but one and did learn a lot.

Some of our show string the next year consisted of those cows I had treated. One was grand champion.

CB was continually on the lookout for animals he could win with. He found a young bull in Canada that had excellent breeding but was small for his age. He was almost a year old when he arrived at the sale barn. CB had me start him back on milk even though he hadn't had any since being weaned months before. He was soon drinking whole milk by the buckets full. He also started growing like a weed. When the Fall show season came, CB wanted a blue ribbon so he could sell him to the bull stud place in Lansing.

Baron was the bull's name. He was not a real big eater, so we substituted milk for a lot of his diet. At the show I would start feeding beet pulp to all the animals early. The bull classes were first, then heifers, then cows.

On show day Baron ate only a little beet pulp and then just stood there. CB was upset. The bull didn't have a large belly to start with, so he needed to eat all he could. CB, as a last resort, had me get two buckets of milk. Baron drank both and away they went to the show ring. He did get first place and bad diarrhea. I had to block our aisle off to the people walking through the barns. He'd shit and it would be like a stream of brown liquid flying clear across the aisle and, boy did it stink!

•

I met many characters during my time at CB's. A lady named Nancy Smith, no relation, had a dairy farm nearby. She was single and could hold her own working with any man. She showed cows too. She hired a herdsman who was an odd ball like her. He and I spent some time together at the shows, but were as different as night and day. To say he was crude was being kind. He was a good worker though. I heard later, after I was back in school, that he had killed himself.

I remember one conversation between CB and Nancy. We were at a cow show and she showed up with lipstick, makeup, etc., which she usually didn't wear. It caught CB by surprise and he blurted out, "You look almost good enough to kiss this morning." Her quick reply, "What do mean almost?" It stopped CB short, but then she smiled and they laughed about it.

There was Herb and Everett Miller; Herb read pedigrees and Everett worked in the sales arena. The other ring man was usually CB's son, CB Jr. Everyone called him Sonny. The other son, John, usually led the cows in the ring. They were both good cowmen and showmen. I didn't envy them having CB for a dad. Trying to live up to the expectations and in the shadow of a man like CB was not easy. My own dad set expectation lots higher then the average dad, so I knew what they faced.

•

I got to attend my first big regional cow show while working for CB. He helped pick out a state herd to take to Chicago in December. A winner there was sure to get mentioned for All-American.

He sent me along to take care of the animals and get them ready for the show. We had animals from several different owners.

My brother George Jr. went with me one year. You had to walk a ways to get to a restaurant. Jr. and I had lamb—we'd never tried it, and we both got sick to our stomach. I have never eaten it since and doubt if George has either.

Everybody wanted CB to lead their animals. His presence could get them a few places higher, they hoped, but this was the big time and not everyone was a fan of CB's.

There were politics involved. I heard all kinds of rumors at the shows, but never knew or cared if any were true. I was learning so much from CB at the time and I had great respect for his knowledge and ability. Nobody's perfect and you can't please everyone—wise old saying! I would learn over the years that my own true motive for things I did or supported could be twisted and misunderstood by others. You do the best you can and the reaction is out of your control.

•

I'll comment on my love life, or lack of it as the case usually was. When I went to CB's I still had pretty strong feelings or maybe just memories for my first real girlfriend, Donna Mae Baker. She was a couple years younger and went to the same country school. Two of my best memories of her and me were when I was able to drive. We went on a date to the Sico Drive-In once. Her parents were in the front seat, Donna, Mike (her brother) and I in the back seat. We'd both cross our arms across or chest so we could hold hands and nobody could see. We'd done that few times before, riding in the teacher's car to a ball game or on a field trip.

Once her parents were having a yard sale. Donna and I volunteered to put up the sign. We took her parents' Buick. I drove the car and there were some tender kisses as we drove the gravel roads and put up the signs. We ended up at different high schools and then I quit school.

We saw each other a few times, but she was dating boys in Dexter High School by then. One was dangerously jealous

The 1960 Chevy convertible

and she ended up marrying him. I stopped one time to see her after she was married and had kids. I just wanted to say hi, but could tell she was afraid to even talk to me as her husband was on the porch. Her family and mine remained friends right up until the time Mom died.

•

My big advantage was having a 1960 Chevy convertible. The first few months I worked for CB I'd have the evenings free. I'd put the top down and cruise Williamston. They had a Dairy Queen, which is where I ate supper. I began to realize that the car was a good "in" with the girls. Sometimes a few would be walking and I'd wave. Sometimes they'd even scream and giggle and wave back. Still I was shy even at twenty years of age.

I came home to CB's one night after I'd moved into the apartment there. It was late fall. They had an auction there sometimes on Saturday nights. CB only rented it for the night. It was kind of like a junk auction. I stood and watched for a little bit. A girl there with her parents kept looking at me and smiling. I finally got up my nerve and went over. We talked and she wanted to see my car, we went out and looked—she got permission from her folks to go for a ride.

She was a senior in high school. We put the top down and the heater on full blast. I made a date for the following Saturday night. We went out a couple of times and she wanted to go steady and wear my ring. I gave it to her but told her about Donna.

She was wearing a dress that night. I wasn't trying to make her jealous, just that Donna had been my only real girlfriend to that point. I had never "gone steady" with anyone else.

All of a sudden she pulled down the top of her dress,

bra and all and exposed her breasts. "Did Donna do this?" she asked. I quickly said no. I was embarrassed by her nerve and just looked. She pulled her dress back up.

We did go steady for a while, but I didn't call as often as I should have, I guess.

I had made friends with a couple of senior boys who worked the cow sales once a month with me. They told me she was dating other boys. I called her and said I'd like to meet and get my ring back. I wasn't in love with her so my feelings weren't hurt. We met and she had my ring on her finger, but I got it back and never saw her again. One unusual thing I remember about her is she'd suck raw eggs through a straw, like you would a milk shake.

·

I had been spending most of my Saturday nights, before coming to Williamston, cruising with my friend Gary Willoughby. He was the one with the '58 Chevy. He was a character and wild by my standards. He had nerve enough for the both of us. He'd see a couple of girls walking and he'd pull over and start talking. Neither of us was very good looking but, with his new car and his gift of gab, they'd usually get in and ride around with us. That's how he met his first wife. She was as nervy as he was. We kept in contact. He called me and said he'd bring me a date for my birthday. He'd met two girls and mine would be a cheerleader from Saline High School. My birthday fell on a Saturday that year so we made our plans. I did my work early so I could get all spiffied up for this girl I'd never met.

I was just finishing up milking and was headed to my apartment when CB's sons, John and Sonny, stopped me. They had this wild first-time heifer and couldn't get the milker on her. They'd hold her, if I'd put the milker on. Sonny covered her head with a bag. He said she couldn't kick cause she couldn't see. John held her tail straight up which kind of paralyzes them. I walked in beside her and hooked the milker to the vacuum line. The second the first suction cup hit her teat, she kicked. If she couldn't see, she sure had a good sense of blind perception.

Her foot hit me in the temple area on the right side of my head. I flew out into the walkway and hit on my ass on the cement. It stunned me for a minute. Then I got mad, which I rarely do. I wasn't going near that cow again and didn't care if she never got milked. I wasn't sure if my head or my ass hurt worse.

•

131 I did go on my date and she was a looker. I don't think she was overly impressed with me and I never saw her again. I didn't date much. I was reading and writing in my free time at night. Some of the area boys I'd met through CB's would come and borrow my car to pick up girls. Luckily, they never got in an accident.

It was stupid of me, but I never gave a thought back then about the lawsuits, etc. that could have resulted. When my brother Carl moved to C.B's we doubled dated once. I remember these two girls wanted to stay out all night. Butch and I had worked all day and had to start milking at 4:30 or 5. We didn't take them out anymore.

The only reason I mention my dating or lack of it is to show the different attitude back then. Girls were expected to draw the line on us boys. I'm not saying what was right or wrong— —just how it was.

I may have been unusual for even those times in that I never slept with anyone until I was married at twenty-four, though my first wife and I did come close just before our marriage. I certainly had opportunity living in my own apartment, but a fear of early pregnancy stopped me, especially having a baby with someone I wasn't sure I'd want to marry.

I was attracted to quiet girls who thought about life. I never chased or hung around the cute, bubbly, popular girls like the other boys did.

•

I recall a small incident where I was questioned by the police and CB came to my rescue. John and Sonny had an office right below my apartment. They sold milking equipment, bulk tanks, etc.

Some one had stolen their petty cash box. Since I lived in the building and had a key to get in the main part, it was only natural to question me. I didn't have a key to any of the offices, just to the main door which led to the stairs.

I was sitting in the back seat of a police car when CB arrived at work. Miss Lynn was already there and filled him in. He came barreling out to the car. The policeman rolled down his window. CB, in his best loud gruff voice declared I had nothing to do with that and we had work to do. I was promptly let out and that was the end of that. I don't recall if they ever discovered who took the cash box. I remember thinking it felt good to know that CB was on my side.

·

I've dislocated both my shoulders three times each. The first time was at CB's. I was clipping a young heifer who wasn't enjoying it. In the scuffle, I tripped over my cord. In attempting to keep from hitting the cement floor, I dislocated my right shoulder.

It's a painful injury. I couldn't get it back in place, so someone drove me to a doctor. He promptly twisted it back in place and put me in a sling.

It's the only time I sought a doctor's help when it happened. I've always been able to get it back in myself. It's a weakness in my arms and is probably worse since I never give the muscles the proper time to heal.

The last time it happened was when my son Adam was born. I was trying to get on top of a float in the pool. I've had some close calls but have been able to avoid either shoulder rolling out again. Knock on wood, because it hurts like hell.

·

In addition to all my reading while I was working at CB's, I also did some writing. I was trying to sound like a professional philosopher using words that Karl Marx had used when describing his ideas on society.

I smile when I read them now. This high school dropout thinking those big thoughts—going to make the world a better place—get people to work together and make life fair for everyone.

Living in the reality of how people are now, I realize how naïve I really was. Education, communication, politics, law––nothing seems to be the answer. No matter the situation, someone is always trying to take advantage, get the upper hand, exploit at someone else's expense. Humans can rationalize anything their minds can conceive – good or bad!

For all my idealism, I still had a firm grip on reality. I knew Ayn Rand's perfect society of intellectual, uncompromising achievers would fall apart within a generation. I knew Karl Marx's utopian society would quickly unravel because of strong inherited traits in us all—mainly greed and ego.

I had no TV and had no urge to get one. I had a radio, but it was mostly silent. I did my job and did it well, but my mind was wrestling with all the uncertainties, inconsistencies and contradictions that seemed to motivate and propel human beings in their struggle to form a stable society.

I grew to appreciate the power of the mind. It had started with Ayn Rand's depiction of characters in her stories that rose above the mundane, trivial average human's thoughts and aspirations.

So strong were my thoughts that I tested them by wearing only a shirt in winter as I drove the tractor to the field to unload the manure. I never got cold. Looking back I realize it was a combination of the power of the mind and the physical toughness of a young man, bent on making a positive change in the world.

On the lighter side... after attending my first State Fair in Detroit caring for CB's show herd, I come face to face with a couple things I had never had. I slept on a cot beside the cows in the dairy barn. Not a real good place to get a night's sleep. I'd shower up on the second floor where the bunkrooms were. Lots of men slept up there, but I wasn't real keen on trading cows mooing all night for men snoring loudly beside me.

After I got home, my feet started to itch and so did my crotch. I'd never heard of Athlete's Foot or crabs – I now had both! Using my dad's cure for everything – iodine and rubbing alcohol, I doused both places. The crabs went away but my feet continued to itch. Between my toes was the worst.

I resorted to my dad's third cure – Epson's salts. I filled a bucket with real warm water added a good dose of Epson's salts and stuck my feet in. It felt good and the itching started to subside. Then, in my enjoyment at the good feeling I flexed my toes. Little did I realize there were hundreds of little cracks in the skin between my toes. The salt went in every one and my feet came out of the bucket.

I rubbed hard between my toes with my fingers to stop the burn of the salt. To my horror, chunks of flesh came off as I rubbed. It scared the hell out of me. I went to the doctor the next day and got the proper medicine. Don't remember what it was because, luckily, I've never had either of those things again. I was a lot more careful in public bathrooms after that!

There should be signs warning naïve farm boys like me about such things.

What I learned at CB's I would use later for our own show string for dad's Whipoorwill Farms. Besides becoming good at clipping and preparing animals for the show ring, I learned CB's way of always showing his animals at their best. Bedding them for their stay at the cow show was an art in itself. Always elevate the front feet and make the animals look as big as possible.

Showing animals at fairs can become addictive, each year filled with hope and anticipation that you'll walk in first place. My brother Carl, who also came to work for CB, got the bug too. My youngest brother, George Jr., didn't until years later when he started showing horses.

In the 1960's black and white dairy shows were in full bloom. There was strong competition between some of the bigger herds. CB always did well because of his eye for picking potential winners. Now very few of those herders are even alive and those that are have become "factory farmers" where individual animals don't matter. It's strictly a business. The cow shows are merely a skeleton of their former glory.

CB had a booming voice, not just loud, but it stood out from everyone else. I remember working a few farm auctions for him. I'd usually be getting the dairy animals ready while CB and his helpers would be selling the tools, and other miscellaneous items. CB would take turns letting his son, CB Jr., and other auctioneers take a turn. I couldn't hear anything for while, then CB would take over again and I could hear every word. That voice made him all the more intimidating.

When it was time to sell the dairy animals, CB never let anyone else have a turn. Even if there were over 200 head, CB auctioned every one of them.

At the sale barn, the ring and auction box were finished in knotty pine. Ropes ran around the ring and fresh shavings covered the dirt floor. Wooden folding chairs would be six or eight rows deep around three sides. CB would be in the auction booth. Miss Lynn was seated to his left. Herb Miller, on CB's right, would read the pedigrees of each registered animal as it was led in.

In each front corner of the ring would be CB Jr. and usually Everett Miller or another man. It was their job to help take bids and keep the pace moving.

CB didn't use a wooden gavel like most auctioneers. He used an old rubber milking inflation. It was the rubber part that fit into a metal sleeve on a milking machine. It was about a foot long.

John Smith, the best showman, would lead the animals in the ring. Everyone except CB and Herb Miller wore white shirts and pants, CB and Herb had on suits.

I can picture it as if it were yesterday. There were pictures on the walls behind CB of the ideal Holstein Dairy cow and bull. Sometimes a small statue of the ideal Holstein cow would sit on the counter by Miss Lynn. A banker from Plymouth had a small table beside the ring and farmers could get instant credit to buy the cows of their choice. My dad used him often. I believe his name was Floyd.

As I've said, CB was just plain intimidating, even more so when he was selling dairy cattle at a fast pace. He kept everyone hopping as animal after animal came walking through the ring.

It was a beautiful sight—the animals, clipped and washed and looking like winners, every one. Most would end up in dairy herds and would never see a clipper or scrub brush again.

That day, they almost glistened as John paraded them around the ring. I remember one day when I had come out to watch a moment. My job was getting animals ready. I'd brush and wipe them down with fly spray or oil just before they went into the ring.

The bids were coming from all sides. CB's eyes roamed the crowd constantly as he took bids and acknowledged those taken by Herb, Everett and C.B. Jr. Everett happened to step in between CB and the bidder he was looking at. "Everett Everett," CB boomed, without missing a beat in his bid taking. Everett literally jumped out of the way. That's how intimidating CB could be.

CB had little patience with people who couldn't make a decision, didn't jump in and do it instead of mulling it over and over. He hated to be interrupted too. One day he was going over registration papers in the barn for some newly arrived cows. He had to match the paper with the drawings of the animals on the back so he'd know who was who. Miss Lynn came out to tell him he had another phone call in the office. It was the third or forth one that morning. I was brushing cows nearby as CB muttered under his breath, "Probably some dumb son of a bitch wants to know how high up is." I've used that saying myself but never out loud.

My urge to write and work at a newspaper was getting stronger. I finally took a day off in the fall of 1961 and drove to Ann Arbor. I went into the *Ann Arbor News* and told them I was looking for a job. I'd start at any task and work my way up as I learned. I admitted to being a high school drop out but assured them my love of writing and journalism was genuine.

The man who interviewed me told me they had graduate students with journalism degrees waiting to get a job there too. As I walked down the hall to leave I could hear them laughing about this "dropout who wanted to be a writer."

I lowered my sights a little and stopped into the offices of the *Chelsea Standard*. Walt Leonard owned it and the *Dexter Leader*, which were weekly newspapers. At least he was polite and urged me to go back and finish high school, then come see him.

I did just that. In January of 1962 I went back to Pioneer High School in Ann Arbor. My cousin Doris Greer's husband's brother was assistant principal there and he got me in even though I should have gone to Dexter where my brothers were attending. I finished my junior and senior year in three semesters but came up a half credit short so still did not get my diploma. I went back to the Chelsea Standard and Walt hired me to sweep floors and cast metal pigs for the linotype machines. More about that in a separate story.

I told CB I was going back to school. He wasn't real happy but gave me some money to help me get started. As I said earlier, it was probably Miss Lynn's idea. My brother Carl was working full time there and took my place as Herdsman.

I wasn't through working at the sale barn how ever. CB had a heart attack that summer. The doctors put him on a diet and some medicine and told him to slow down—that fell on deaf ears however. CB could not slow down.

At an auction—I think in the spring of 1962 CB had another heart attack and died. His widow called me and asked if I would come get the herd ready to be sold. I took a week off school and went back to Williamston. I didn't attend the funeral because CB did not look like the same person I'd worked for. I saw him at a regular monthly auction a few months before he died and he looked awful.

We sold his herd. The day of the sale, as I did my old job of getting the cattle ready before they went into the sale ring, I suddenly pictured CB in the auction box, both hands in the air, one holding the rubber inflation, the other with one finger outstretched. He'd done it hundreds of times. He used that gesture as he gave the buyers one last chance to bid before bring both arms down and bellowing, "Sold."

I walked back out into the barn so no one would see the tears rolling down both cheeks. He was one of a kind, a true individual and one of the bosses I respected the most.

The sale barn had been sold to Casey. He lasted a while, then the empire CB had built slowly slipped away. The old sale barn became a landscape, lawn mower sales business. The big barn slowly deteriorated away.

At that point in my life I am lucky that our paths crossed. CB will be part of my good memories until I'm gone too.

Lesson in life — a journey south

History books we study through the first eight grades are glaringly short on details when it comes to the way things really were. Our American history is full of short stories about famous people and events. It accents the positive and, for young children forming their first opinions of the culture they were born into, that's probably best. Plenty of time later for reality to come thundering over us as we stand innocently in the middle of the road. That was especially true for this farm boy born in 1940.

Newspapers were never delivered to our door. TV didn't enter my life until the early '50s. The only radio I was familiar with was the weekly "Lone Ranger" program, which I listened to by sitting on the floor with one ear against the speaker.

•

The setting for my childhood was a 210-acre farm nestled amongst a mostly German rural community. White, Protestant, hard working farm families were the only real culture I experienced. I was privileged to be born when and where I was. All these years later, having long ago lost my idealized visions of American and its people, I still feel that way. They had not created the prejudice I would encounter. How much they were even aware of it at the time I can only guess. They were people who minded their own business and only got involved in what they realistically had a chance to change. I was taught by example to respect those around me and the importance of self-respect which could only be achieved by setting self-imposed standards. The only people looked down on or openly criticized were a couple of men who drank too much or were abusive to their wives—the latter unforgivable in an atmosphere where women were considered the smart ones.

Until I attended junior high school, I had only encountered one black family. They were farmers and lived in a nearby small town. If there was racial prejudice of any kind toward them, I was unaware of it. In junior high in Ann Arbor in 1953 there were a large number of black kids in school. A black teen named Jim Turner was elected class president. One of my close friends, Lottle Fonvile was black. If there were racial undercurrents, I was again unaware of those too.

The only kids I remember who formed their own little "outside" group were ones we called "hoods". They wore their collars up, had duck-bill haircuts and home-made tattoos on their arms. These were tattoos they acquired at school recess while we watched in awe as they unflinchingly suffered from the poking of a plain sewing needle and ink pen.

Slavery and North and South were just short chapters already covered in my history class. It had happened long ago––just a footnote in history like Napoleon or our own fight for independence. We were just plain Americans now, "Yankees" only to people in foreign countries.

I got my first away-from-home full-time job in 1960. It was for an auctioneer who among many other things, purchased truckloads of young milk cows to send south and west to the dairy herds there. That's how I ended up in the cab of a trailer headed for Baton Rouge, Louisiana. There were two trailers full of cattle. My job was to accompany the cows to the fair grounds, set up the auction ring and wash and groom them. The auctioneer would arrive in a few days to sell them individually to the dairymen of that area.

I was already aware that many restroom signs still read "white only" and "colored". I'd seen them on a trip to Florida with two friends on spring break in high school a few years before. We had seen them, paused and looked at each other, but dutifully entered the "whites only" without comment.

Here, in 1960, the civil rights unrest had already begun. I did not watch TV during those years of living alone. I read a lot: books about history, culture, etc. I was trying to understand the real world that history had not prepared me for. More than that, I was trying to understand how human beings did the things they did, Hitler and Germany being a recent example of what man is capable of. I was only vaguely aware of the protest marches and events in the South. I would soon come face to face with human attitudes and prejudice that I had not witnessed in the basically white community I'd grown up in.

Arriving in Baton Rouge, we or I should say I, unloaded the cows before an audience of people who were officials or bystanders at the fairgrounds. I had to individually lead each cow off the truck and tie it in the area they had designated. No one watching nor the truck driver offered to help. When I'd finished, I let the cows rest for the next several hours. A man in a white suit showed me the arena and where it was to be set up. I'd already figured out that I was surrounded by lookers, not workers, I learned later many of those watching were on the sale committee sponsoring the dairy sale.

It was hot, but I do well physically in the heat so I set about setting posts, etc. One man finally asked if I needed help.

I told him yes, since a lot to hard work was ahead just getting the cattle trimmed and washed before sale day. "I'll get you some," and he walked off. He soon returned with four or five black men. "Jus' tell 'em what to do and keep an eye on 'em," were his instructions.

I looked at these men. Every face had the look of a man resigned to second-class citizenship. It shocked me.

I started explaining what had to be done. Part of the work was leveling the area where the arena would rest. I had been already shoveling when they'd arrived. A whole cart full of hand tools was nearby. While the others went to get a shovel or a pick, one man tried to take my shovel. I realized he was expecting them to do the work while I stood by and supervised.

No man did that where I grew up. We all worked side by side and equally. I told the man trying to take my shovel that they were there to help, not take over my job. I made them all nervous, I could sense. They kept looking over at the lookers as we worked. I didn't need to look; I could feel the disapproval from the white onlookers. I didn't care. I was already pretty sure of who I was and I was not a man who stood and watched other people do my work. Not one word was spoken by any of my black co-workers. I'd explained and showed them what needed to be done and we did it. Most of the on-lookers had drifted away by the time we finished setting up the sale arena. I thanked the black men for helping. I saw something else in their faces now. It was the look of men who knew that I respected them and that in my eyes they were equals. It was a look that I've remembered ever since and it made me even surer I'd done right.

I was not a civil rights activist. I would not have joined these men in a protest march or sit-in even if they'd asked me. That also went against the individuality I'd grown up to respect. If I had a problem, my parents had taught me to deal with it, not look to a committee or government to solve it.

As I watched the ugliness unfold over the next several years, I realized what power pent up emotions have when they're finally released. I did not agree with the rioting and lawlessness. I could not justify the means to an end where there would be equal harmony. I understood the goals; the methods seemed too divisive to ever achieve them.

By the time the rioting hit my home state of Michigan, I was back in the little town I'd been born near, working for a weekly newspaper. The rioting finally hit Ann Arbor, the town where I had gone to school, where my only black high school friend, Lottle Fonvil lived. An inner battle was brewing between my belief in the equality of all people and the belief that the marches and rioting were self-defeating, alienating many people who had always believed in equal rights. What were those marchers hoping to achieve? What did I have as a white person that I could give them? What could any race of people give another? They seemed to be talking about material things from housing to wages. The rioters were taking things they could not afford to buy, but at what price to their character, their culture as a people. Respect? That can't be passed out like candy; it's earned, by each individual one at a time.

When a planned march was announced through downtown Ann Arbor, I paced the floor of my print shop practicing a speech I would give to the marchers. How would I get them to listen? How could I make my point that material things are not the benchmark of a people, that far more was at stake here than equal pay or housing?

They were risking their future reputation. They would be viewed as takers and demanders, not achievers. That would be devastating to them as a people in the long term. Those were my thoughts as I paced the floor.

I did come up with a way of getting the marchers' attention. I wonder what paths my life would have taken had I dared follow through. I pictured myself walking out into the street in front of them, stripping my clothes completely off and saying. "Here is a white man, what have I got that you don't? What can I give you? My clothes? Take them. My shoes? Take them. You are seeking my respect, self-confidence, and status? I can't give those even if I wanted too. You have everything important that I have, arms, legs, eyes, a brain. Those are the things I use to be who I am. You all have those things already."

What ultimately stopped my fantasy folly was the realization that they would not understand what I was trying to say. All I would accomplish would be to embarrass my family and myself. I also wasn't sure if the marchers would laugh at my skinny naked frame or beat me up for daring to question their motives. With large groups of people bent on making a statement, things can get ugly in a hurry. As is shown repeatedly, a group of friendly, law abiding citizens can turn into an uncontrollable, unreasonable, mob when group mentality takes over.

I settled instead for calling Lottle and asking him to meet with me. We hadn't seen each other in over ten years. I had quit school at sixteen and helped on the farm, then gone back and finished twelfth grade when I was twenty-two. He had finished and had a family now.

We met in Ann Arbor. I wanted, most of all, to understand not only the motive for the civil rights marches, but what they hoped for as the end result. In my own mind at the time, any ultimate solution that didn't bring harmony and understanding between the two races was self-defeating. If a black family gained equal pay, equal opportunity to purchase a house anywhere they desired but were still treated with distrust and suspicion by their white neighbors, nothing of real value had been gained.

I would realize over time what an idealistic, unrealistic vision I had for racial harmony. Still, I would also see by the late 1980's that a generation of black kids, forced by law into white schools, taught and passed from grade to grade by teachers who did not want to teach them, had gained a hollow victory. They walked out with a diploma but were still unable to read and write.

Time and events had changed Lottle as they had me. I could tell he was now a little suspicious of the motives behind my questions. We had never discussed racial issues when we were in school. I realized he had been almost as naïve as I about the real underlying racial divide in America. He related the changes in his own life since the riots and marches had begun. For the first time in his life, he felt he had been stopped and questioned by the police simply because he was young, black and out late at night. This had happened more than once in the past few months. There was an unpleasant edge to his voice at the unfairness of it.

As I drove home later, I was even more unsure of the wisdom of forcing the racial issue no matter how overdue equal rights was. While there were hundreds of looters and thousands of marchers, there were millions of black people like Lottle who had done neither. They would silently reap the rewards if the civil rights movement was successful and likewise suffer the consequences of two peoples increasingly hostile toward each other.

People in the community I lived in were growing increasingly frustrated at understanding what blacks wanted, what they hoped to gain. As weeks and months went by and major cities one-by-one dealt with the violence, the frustration turned to resentment and then to open hostility toward blacks in general. People whom I had never heard say a negative thing about black people were now openly and blatantly critical. Was racism always there, hidden beneath the surface? Was prejudice just as bad in the North—only more subtle? I remember reading that statement by Southerners feeling the sting of criticism from Northern civil rights advocates.

It seemed to me there was one difference. In the North blacks were judged individually; they at least had a fighting chance at equal treatment. In the South, in the Sixties, skin color alone automatically stereotyped them as second-class citizens no matter their work ethic, material success or social interaction.

Over the years, I've observed all kinds of prejudices, including some of my own. I've concluded that at the base of those feelings is not skin color or ethnic background. These are just the outer, easily identifiable features that allow us to stereotype people. At the root of prejudice is suspicion, a misperception that the motives, goals, values, etc., of another individual or groups are at cross-purpose to our own. The things that are critically important to us are not to them. Those core feelings are reflected in our attitudes. It is attitudes that give us our first impression.

As I listened to the growing resentment of people around me in the Sixties toward blacks, I first realized it wasn't really color or race. It was suspicion and resentment based on the growing belief that blacks did not share the same ideals, the same middle class work ethic, the same individual initiative as we did. They weren't here to earn their share of the American dream, they were here to exploit it, or worse, maybe even destroy it all together. They obviously didn't appreciate that we all earned our way of life by the freedom of individual initiative.

The common ground that bound us together in mutual respect and purpose was eroding from under out feet. Only in my quiet personal thoughts did I question the accuracy of that conclusion, yet how often is a perceived view, oblivious to facts, taken at face value.

Unfortunately, very often, we are quick to condemn if it suits our own purpose.   Viewing the angry mobs, the burning buildings, it was easy to dismiss the many thousands of blacks who were working every day toward the American Dream, dealing with handicaps I could not even imagine.

I did my job well, the sale was a success and everyone was happy. The impact of seeing first-hand the effect of years of prejudice on the faces of those black men who helped me has stuck with me all these years.

No human face should reflect an inner feeling of inferiority. We have varying talents, different natural abilities. We should all have the right to give it our best shot, free of prejudice.

That's the lesson I learned.

Macombers with harness on wooden horse exhibit:
Left to right: Harry, Barbara, Carl, George Jr.,
(w/George's son in front) Shirley, Linda

The Macomber farm house in October 2005

Author's Note:

My profound apologies to English teachers everywhere. The grammar, sentence structure and spelling errors are solely my responsibility. These stories were all written longhand in barely legible form. Through hours of hard work by Julie Leonard, to whom I am forever indebted, they appear in typed format so I can share them with you. In fact, all but the actual printing is a result of volunteer effort on everyone's part.

I, who lived these stories and you, who read them, are among the very privileged few. Life is not fair for so many others who inhabit this planet with us. It is my sincerest wish that future generations will strive even harder until some day everyone will share in what we so selfishly take for granted.

And finally, to any English teachers who might read these lines, while I might deserve a failing grade for composition, I'm hoping for a C+ or better for content.

Harry Macomber

The author with his dad, George, in 1992

Harry Macomber
212 Barrett Rd
Watertown, TN 37184
harrymac@dtccom.net

Made in the USA